state capital

animals

JUMBLE®

BrainBusters

Junior

Because Learning Can Be Fun!

outer space

David L. Hoyt
and
Russell L. Hoyt

human body

sports

money

TRIUMPH
BOOKS
CHICAGO

This book is available at special discounts
for your group or organization.

For further information, contact:

Triumph Books
601 South LaSalle Street
Suite 500
Chicago, Illinois 60605
(312) 939-3330
(312) 663-3557 FAX

ISBN 1-892049-29-5

Printed in the USA

CONTENTS

state capitals

animals

JUMBLE

BrainBusters

Junior

BEGINNER
PUZZLES

human body

outer space

money

sports

U.S. STATE CAPITALS

JUMBLE BrainBusters! Junior

Unscramble the Jumbles, one letter to each square, to spell U.S. state capitals.

#1 EEHANL
Helen g

#2 EUAJUN
Juneau

Montgomery
Juneau
Phoenix
Little Rock
Sacramento
Denver
Hartford
Dover
Tallahassee
Atlanta
Honolulu
Boise
Springfield
Indianapolis
Des Moines
Topeka
Frankfort

Baton Rouge
Augusta
Annapolis
Boston
Lansing
St. Paul
Jackson
Jefferson City
Helena
Lincoln
Carson City
Concord
Trenton
Santa Fe
Albany
Raleigh
Bismarck

Columbus
Oklahoma City
Salem
Harrisburg
Providence
Columbia
Pierre
Nashville
Austin
Salt Lake City
Montpelier
Richmond
Olympia
Charleston
Madison
Cheyenne

#3 TATNAAL
Atlanta

#4 RENTONT
Trenton

#5 PLYIAMO
Olympia

Arrange the circled letters
to solve the mystery answer.

MYSTERY ANSWER
Honolulu

Box of Clues

Stumped? Maybe you can find a clue below.

-Georgia   -Hawaii
-Alaska   -Washington
-New Jersey   -Montana

THE HUMAN BODY

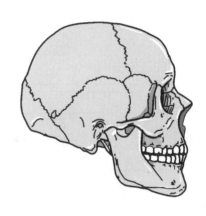

Unscramble the Jumbles, one letter to each square, to spell words related to the human body.

#1 HRIA

H a i (r)

#2 EHDA

H e (a) d

#3 OEBN

B (o) n e

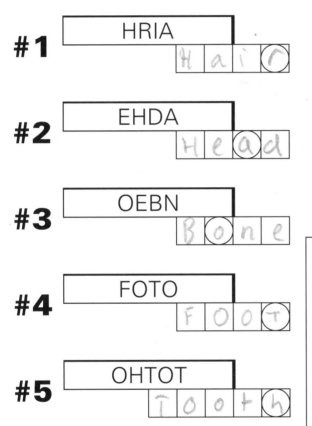

#4 FOTO

F O O (T)

Interesting Human Body Facts

The thumbnail is the slowest growing of the fingernails.

There are trillions of cells in the human body.

#5 OHTOT

T o o t (h)

#6 UTBMH

(T) h u m b

Arrange the circled letters to solve the mystery answer.

MYSTERY ANSWER

r a o t h T

NOUNS

Unscramble the Jumbles, one letter
to each square, to spell nouns.

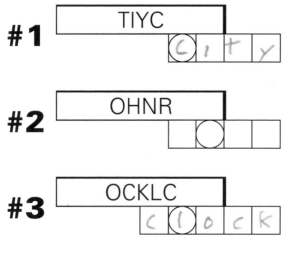

#1 TIYC
C i t y

#2 OHNR

#3 OCKLC
c l o c k

#4 OTHTO
T o o t h

#5 CIUSM

#6 NOMHT
M o n t h

Arrange the circled letters
to solve the mystery answer.

"Animal"
"Dinosaur"
"Reptile"

"Runner"
"Athlete"
"Racer"

"Tree"
"Plant"
"Cypress"

A noun is *a word that is the name
of something (as in a person, animal,
place, thing, quality, idea or action).*

Box of Clues

Stumped? Maybe you can find a clue
below.

-Molar, for example
-Timepiece
-Large town
-One year divided by 12
-Teacher work area
-Car noisemaker
-Combinations of notes

MYSTERY ANSWER

ELEMENTS

JUMBLE BrainBusters! Junior

Unscramble the Jumbles, one letter to each square, to spell names of elements.

THE PERIODIC TABLE

#1 RNIO

I r o n

#2 ORONB

B o r o n

#3 BCATLO

#4 OSIDMU

S o d i u m

#5 LACIMUC
c a l c i u m

Arrange the circled letters to solve the mystery answer.

MYSTERY ANSWER

Name		
Actinium	Gold	Potassium
Aluminum	Hafnium	Praseodymium
Americium	Hassium	Promethium
Antimony	Helium	Protactinium
Argon	Holmium	Radium
Arsenic	Hydrogen	Radon
Astatine	Indium	Rhenium
Barium	Iodine	Rhodium
Berkelium	Iridium	Rubidium
Beryllium	Iron	Ruthenium
Bismuth	Krypton	Rutherfordium
Bohrium	Lanthanum	Samarium
Boron	Lawrencium	Scandium
Bromine	Lead	Seaborgium
Cadmium	Lithium	Selenium
Calcium	Lutetium	Silicon
Californium	Magnesium	Silver
Carbon	Manganese	Sodium
Cerium	Meitnerium	Strontium
Cesium	Mendelevium	Sulfur
Chlorine	Mercury	Tantalum
Chromium	Molybdenum	Technetium
Cobalt	Neodymium	Tellurium
Copper	Neon	Terbium
Curium	Neptunium	Thallium
Dubnium	Nickel	Thorium
Dysprosium	Niobium	Thulium
Einsteinium	Nitrogen	Tin
Erbium	Nobelium	Titanium
Europium	Osmium	Tungsten
Fermium	Oxygen	Uranium
Fluorine	Palladium	Vanadium
Francium	Phosphorus	Xenon
Gadolinium	Platinum	Ytterbium
Gallium	Plutonium	Yttrium
Germanium	Polonium	Zinc
	Potassium	Zirconium

MATH

JUMBLE BrainBusters! Junior

Unscramble the Jumbled
letters, one letter to each square,
so that each equation is correct.

For example: NONTEOEOW
ONE + ONE = TWO

#1 OTRWOTOUWF

t w o + t w o = F o u r

#2 VFIFVEEEINT

☐☐☐◯☐ + ☐☐☐◯☐ = ◯☐☐☐

#3 GEITNIOHNNEE

☐☐☐☐☐☐ + ☐☐◯ = ☐☐☐◯☐

#4 EFRUHROTEOEN

☐☐◯☐☐ − ☐◯☐☐☐☐ = ◯☐☐

#5 HTRREEREZOHEET

☐☐◯☐☐ + ☐☐☐◯☐ = ☐☐◯☐☐

Arrange the circled letters
to solve the mystery equation.

MYSTERY EQUATION

◯◯◯ + ◯◯◯◯◯ = ◯◯◯◯

ANIMALS

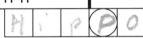

Unscramble the Jumbles, one letter
to each square, to spell names of
animals.

#1 POIHP
H i p p o

#2 OOMES
M o o s e

#3 YRUETK
T u r k e y

#4 LAUWSR
W a r u s

#5 AIRGFEF
G I R A F F E

#6 ECICHNK
C h i c k e n

Arrange the circled letters
to solve the mystery answer.

MYSTERY ANSWER

PETELAHN

STARTS WITH "C"

Unscramble the Jumbles, one letter to each square, to spell words that start with "C".

#1 ROCNW

#2 CODWR

#3 STCCUA

#4 FCEOFE

#5 MCILXA

#6 AACPILT

Arrange the circled letters to solve the mystery answer.

Box of Clues

Stumped? Maybe you can find a clue below.

- Large group of people
- Austin, to Texas
- Relating to the middle
- Highest point
- _____ break
- Type of plant
- Headgear

MYSTERY ANSWER

MUSICAL INSTRUMENTS

Unscramble the Jumbles, one letter to each square, to spell names of musical instruments.

#1 AHPR

#2 LFUET
F l u t e

#3 NABOJ

#4 TUIRAG

#5 CIPOOCL

#6 ERUTPTM

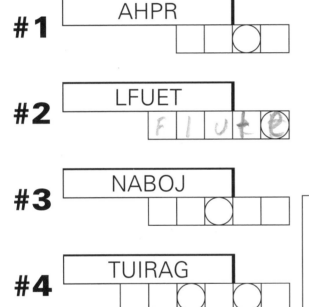

Box of Clues

Stumped? Maybe you can find a clue below.

-Small flute
-Type of woodwind
-Stringed instrument with a triangle frame
-Stringed instrument
-Type of woodwind
-Wind instrument with a flared end
-Stringed instrument

Arrange the circled letters to solve the mystery answer.

MYSTERY ANSWER

FOOD

Unscramble the Jumbles, one letter to each square, to spell words related to food.

JUMBLE BrainBusters! Junior

#1 ZIAPZ

P i z z a

#2 OSTAT

#3 USARG

s u g a r

#4 NACYD

Box of Clues

Stumped? Maybe you can find a clue below.

-Sweet additive
-Cheese _____
-Heated sliced bread
-Movie food
-Round food
-Sweet snack food
-Dill _____

#5 ODTUN

#6 CPIELK

P i c k l e

Arrange the circled letters to solve the mystery answer.

MYSTERY ANSWER

U.S. STATES

Unscramble the Jumbles, one letter to each square, to spell names of U.S. states.

#1 HOIO

O H I O

#2 DIOHA

I d a h o

#3 AIEMN

M a i n e

#4 VEAADN

N e v a d a

#5 AKASNS

K a n s a s

Box of Clues

Stumped? Maybe you can find a clue below.

-Home to Boise
-Home to Cleveland and Cincinnati
-Largest New England state
-Home to Las Vegas
-Home to Indianapolis
-Home to Topeka

Arrange the circled letters to solve the mystery answer.

MYSTERY ANSWER

I n d i a n a

IAIDNNA

C Hacca Hoca

SPORTS

Unscramble the Jumbles, one letter
to each square, to spell words related
to sports.

#1 OLFU
f o u l

#2 TCHAC
c a t c h

#3 OCCHA
c o a c h

#4 NXIGBO
b o x i n g

#5 LACTEK

#6 SBETAK

Box of Clues

Stumped? Maybe you can find a clue
below.

-NBA player's target
-Leader, trainer
-Outfielder's goal
-H.A.'s and B.R.'s sport
-Muhammad Ali's sport
-Break a rule
-Bring to the ground

Arrange the circled letters
to solve the mystery answer.

MYSTERY ANSWER

WEATHER

Unscramble the Jumbles, one letter to each square, to spell words related to weather.

#1 AMRW

#2 RFOTN

#3 USNYN

#4 GFGYO

#5 LCILYH

#6 REZFEE

Arrange the circled letters to solve the mystery answer.

Interesting Weather Facts

Vanguard II was the first satellite to send weather information back to Earth from space (1959).

Oak Ridge, Tenn., is considered the least windiest city in the U.S. with an average wind speed of just more than 4 mph.

MYSTERY ANSWER

U.S. PRESIDENTS

JUMBLE BrainBusters! Junior

Unscramble the Jumbles, one letter to each square, to spell last names of U.S. presidents.

#1 TTFA

#2 YEHAS

#3 NRGTA

#4 LATYRO

#5 AHIDNRG

#6 RRIHONSA

Arrange the circled letters to solve the mystery answer.

PRESIDENTS OF THE UNITED STATES OF AMERICA

1789-1797 George Washington	1889-1893 Benjamin Harrison
1797-1801 John Adams	1893-1897 Grover Cleveland
1801-1809 Thomas Jefferson	1897-1901 William McKinley
1809-1817 James Madison	1901-1909 Theodore (Teddy) Roosevelt
1817-1825 James Monroe	1909-1913 William Howard Taft
1825-1829 John Quincy Adams	1913-1921 Thomas Woodrow Wilson
1829-1837 Andrew Jackson	1921-1923 Warren G. Harding
1837-1841 Martin Van Buren	1923-1929 John Calvin Coolidge
1841 William Henry Harrison	1929-1933 Herbert Hoover
1841-1845 John Tyler	1933-1945 Franklin D. Roosevelt
1845-1849 James Polk	1945-1953 Harry S. Truman
1849-1850 Zachary Taylor	1953-1961 Dwight David Eisenhower
1850-1853 Millard Fillmore	1961-1963 John Fitzgerald Kennedy
1853-1857 Franklin Pierce	1963-1969 Lyndon B. Johnson
1857-1861 James Buchanan	1969-1974 Richard M. Nixon
1861-1865 Abraham Lincoln	1974-1977 Gerald R. Ford
1865-1869 Andrew Johnson	1977-1981 James (Jimmy) Carter
1869-1877 Ulysses S. Grant	1981-1989 Ronald Reagan
1877-1881 Rutherford B. Hayes	1989-1993 George W. Bush
1881 James A. Garfield	1993-2001 William Jefferson Clinton
1881-1885 Chester A. Arthur	2001- George Walker Bush
1885-1889 Stephen Grover Cleveland	

Box of Clues

Stumped? Maybe you can find a clue below.

#1- 27th U.S. president
#2- U.S. president 1877-1881
#3- President on the $50 bill
#4- This president fought in the War of 1812
#5- This president died while in office
#6- Ninth U.S. president
M.A.- This president fought in the Civil War

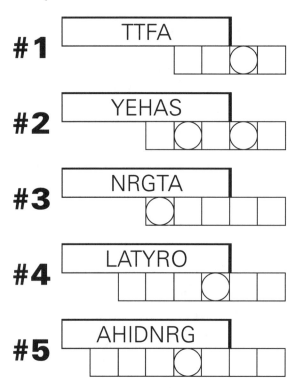

MYSTERY ANSWER

COUNTRIES

Unscramble the Jumbles, one letter to each square, to spell names of countries.

#1 HIELC

#2 SURIAS

#3 RZIBLA

#4 RUETYK

#5 AAADNC

#6 CEIOXM

Box of Clues

Stumped? Maybe you can find a clue below.

- Skinny South American country
- Home to the Baja Peninsula
- Largest country
- Home to Melbourne
- Largest South American country
- This country shares its name with a bird

MYSTERY ANSWER

Arrange the circled letters to solve the mystery answer.

STARTS WITH A VOWEL

Unscramble the Jumbles, one letter to each square, to spell words that start with vowels (a,e,i,o,u).

#1  AITYL

#2  GIOOL

#3  EALYL

#4  ELORD

#5  EWAKA

#6 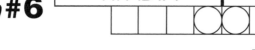 RFADIA

Box of Clues

Stumped? Maybe you can find a clue below.

- Scared
- Conscious
- Northern home
- European country
- Not allowed
- Bowling _____
- Around longer

Arrange the circled letters to solve the mystery answer.

MYSTERY ANSWER

PLANET EARTH

Unscramble the Jumbles, one letter
to each square, to spell words related
to planet Earth.

#1 LHIL

#2 ADLN

#3 VRIRE

#4 RCTSU

#5 LVLAYE

#6 GLAONO

Box of Clues

Stumped? Maybe you can find a clue
below.

-Low land between two hills
-Small mountain
-Flowing body of water
-Surrounded land
-Earth's outermost solid part
-Shallow channel or sound
 connected to a larger body
 of water
-Solid ground

Arrange the circled letters
to solve the mystery answer.

MYSTERY ANSWER

STARTS WITH "F"

Unscramble the Jumbles, one letter
to each square, to words that start
with "F".

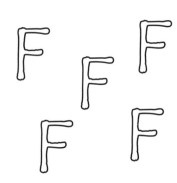

#1 TFHIG

#2 CFOKL

#3 LOFRO

#4 ZROFNE

#5 LACFNO

#6 EFEDMOR

Box of Clues

Stumped? Maybe you can find a clue
below.

-Frigid
-Base
-Group of animals
-Brawl
-Scandinavian country
-Type of bird
-Independence

Arrange the circled letters
to solve the mystery answer.

MYSTERY ANSWER

LARGE CITIES

JUMBLE. BrainBusters! Junior

Unscramble the Jumbles, one letter to each square, to spell names of large cities.

#1 ACIOR

#2 REBINL

#3 NLONOD

#4 DMIDRA

#5 TRDTIOE

#6 TALAANT

Box of Clues

Stumped? Maybe you can find a clue below.

- _____, Spain (starts with "M")
- _____, Egypt (starts with "C")
- _____, U.S.A. (starts with "D")
- _____, England (starts with "L")
- _____, Canada (starts with "T")
- _____, U.S.A. (starts with "A")
- _____, Germany (starts with "B")

Arrange the circled letters to solve the mystery answer.

MYSTERY ANSWER

COUNTRIES

JUMBLE BrainBusters! Junior

Unscramble the Jumbles, one letter to each square, to spell names of countries.

#1 UCAB

#2 YLIAB

#3 USIASR

#4 NOAPDL

#5 TINMAEV

#6 NGRAYEM

Arrange the circled letters to solve the mystery answer.

MYSTERY ANSWER

MEANS THE SAME

JUMBLE. BrainBusters! Junior

Unscramble the Jumbles, one letter to each square, to spell pairs of words with the same or similar meanings.

For example:

| HYSIN | | BGRTIH |
| S H I N Y | | B R I G H T |

#1 OHEM   HOSEU

#2 TOSF   ETNGLE

#3 RPIEZ   RAADW

#4 RPDIA   SEDEYP

#5 ALUHG   CLKECA

Arrange the circled letters to solve the mystery answer.

MYSTERY ANSWER

21

BASKETBALL

Unscramble the Jumbles, one letter to each square, to spell words related to basketball.

#1 UOFL

#2 RGADU

#3 EEJSYR

#4 SABETK

#5 NELPTYA

#6 FENFESO

Interesting Basketball Facts

Spalding has estimated that an average NBA basketball has a lifespan of about 10,000 bounces.

A basketball hoop is 18 inches in diameter.

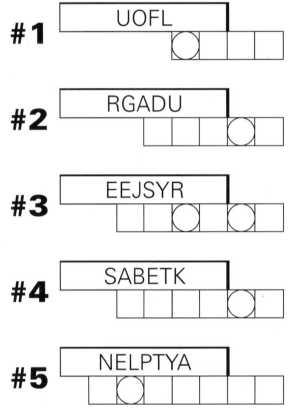

Arrange the circled letters to solve the mystery answer.

MYSTERY ANSWER

RHYMES

Unscramble the Jumbles, one letter to each square, to spell pairs of rhyming words.

JUMBLE BrainBusters! Junior

For example:

LBPIM → B L I M P ═══ MIPCH → C H I M P

#1 ABLKC → ATCKR

#2 UCHLN → NUHBC

#3 NKCKO → CTSOK

#4 AHITB → BARITB

#5 EGHED → GELDPE

Arrange the circled letters to solve the mystery answer.

MYSTERY ANSWER

OUTER SPACE

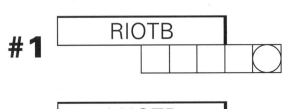

Unscramble the Jumbles, one letter to each square, to spell words related to outer space.

#1 RIOTB

#2 LUOTP

#3 CTEOM

#4 RSNUAT

#5 AUUSNR

#6 UIERJTP

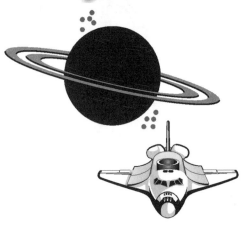

Box of Clues

Stumped? Maybe you can find a clue below.

-Tailed orbiter
-Outermost planet (on average)
-Largest planet
-Home to Triton (moon)
-Ringed planet
-Moon's path
-Seventh planet

Arrange the circled letters to solve the mystery answer.

MYSTERY ANSWER

STARTS WITH "G"

Unscramble the Jumbles, one letter to each square, to spell words that start with "G".

#1 AGUIRT

#2 CGEREE

#3 RGDONU

#4 MALGEB

#5 PRUYGM

#6 RHOGWT

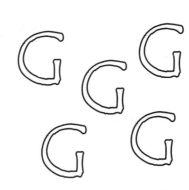

Box of Clues

Stumped? Maybe you can find a clue below.

- -Earth's solid surface
- -Irritable
- -Trash
- -Development
- -European country
- -A musical instrument
- -Wager, risk

Arrange the circled letters to solve the mystery answer.

MYSTERY ANSWER

TIME LINE

Unscramble the Jumbles, one letter to each square, to spell words as suggested by the time line.

#1 1947 First supersonic _____

#1 GLIHTF

#2 1954 _____ divided into North and South

#2 ATEVMIN

#3 1961 _____ becomes U.S. president

#3 NENKDYE

#4 1981 Martial law declared in _____

#4 LONPDA

#5 1990 Iraq invades _____

#5 WUIKTA

#6 1991 Boris Yeltsin becomes president of _____

#6 USRIAS

Arrange the circled letters to solve the mystery answer. **1949** The creation of East and West _____

MYSTERY ANSWER ○○○○○○○○

POETRY

Unscramble the Jumbles, one letter to each square, to spell words found in the poem.

#1 REILCDHN

#2 TUPWON

#3 PPLEEO

#4 OEHM

#5 NWIRET

WINTER'S ARRIVAL
by Kim Nolan

A blustery wind blows
All through our town
_____ #1 look up
As snow falls down

_____ #2 and downtown
_____ #3 begin to scurry
They rush to get _____ #4
It's beginning to flurry

Sidewalks get shoveled
Snow plows appear
Get out your parkas
_____ #5 is here

Arrange the circled letters to solve the mystery answer. (The mystery answer is not in the poem.)

MYSTERY ANSWER

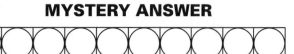

THE HUMAN BODY

JUMBLE BrainBusters! Junior

Unscramble the Jumbles, one letter to each square, to spell words related to the human body.

#1 NAHD

#2 NAELK

#3 ECTHS

#4 UOHTM

#5 EKDYIN

#6 MOSAHTC

Box of Clues

Stumped? Maybe you can find a clue below.

- Bean-shaped organ
- Low arm part
- Food digestion area
- Heart and lung area
- Frame
- Type of joint
- Tongue's area

Arrange the circled letters to solve the mystery answer.

MYSTERY ANSWER

ADJECTIVES

Unscramble the Jumbles, one letter
to each square, to spell adjectives.

#1 HRIC

#2 YITN

#3 EINC

#4 LATL

#5 OSTF

#6 OBDL

"Bright"
"Sunny"
"Warm"

"Large"
"African"
"Asian"

*"Strong"
"Muscular"
"Powerful"*

An adjective is a word that modifies
a noun by describing it. An adjective
might indicate a noun's quantity or
extent, or specify a thing as distinct
from something else.

Arrange the circled letters
to solve the mystery answer.

MYSTERY ANSWER

Box of Clues

Stumped? Maybe you can find a clue
below.

-Describe a brave or fearless
person
-Describe a person with a lot
of money
-Describe melting ice cream
-Describe the average NBA
player
-Describe an atom
-Describe a piece of fruit that
is too ripe to eat
-Describe a friendly person

ALL ABOUT MONEY

Unscramble the Jumbles, one letter to each square, to spell words related to money.

#1 ACHS

#2 AVUTL

#3 EHCKC

#4 NEPYN

#5 RLODLA

#6 ACREGH

Box of Clues

Stumped? Maybe you can find a clue below.

-Lincoln's coin
-Storage area
-U.S. currency
-Accepted money used as medium of exchange
-Pay later
-Written order for payment
-Coins and bills

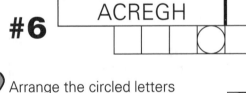

Arrange the circled letters to solve the mystery answer.

MYSTERY ANSWER

ALL ABOUT PLANTS

Unscramble the Jumbles, one letter to each square, to spell words related to plants.

#1 ESDE

#2 EFNR

#3 RTNUK

#4 OLBMO

Box of Clues

Stumped? Maybe you can find a clue below.

-Pine _____
-Main stem of a tree
-Plant beginning
-Forest
-Flower part
-Orchid or azalea
-Spore producing, vascular plant

#5 OSOWD

#6 EELNED

Arrange the circled letters to solve the mystery answer.

MYSTERY ANSWER

STARTS WITH "H"

Unscramble the Jumbles, one letter to each square, to spell words that start with "H".

#1 PHYPA

#2 UOSHE

#3 NUHRTE

#4 OHTRET

#5 HMEARM

#6 AOHLIYD

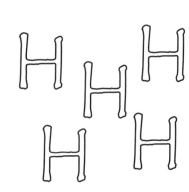

Box of Clues

Stumped? Maybe you can find a clue below.

-Home
-Warmer
-Small rodent
-Special day
-Joyous
-Pounding instrument
-Seeker

Arrange the circled letters to solve the mystery answer.

MYSTERY ANSWER

U.S. CITIES

Unscramble the Jumbles, one letter to each square, to spell names of U.S. cities.

#1 TNOBOS

#2 HOPIXNE

#3 ACIHOGC

#4 TESALET

#5 FUABLOF

#6 NRODAOL

Box of Clues

Stumped? Maybe you can find a clue below.

-City in New York near
 Niagara Falls
-Home to the Red Sox
-Central Florida city
-Largest Texas city
-Illinois city on Lake
 Michigan
-Largest Arizona city
-Washington city on Puget
 Sound

Arrange the circled letters to solve the mystery answer.

MYSTERY ANSWER

ANIMALS

Unscramble the Jumbles, one letter to each square, to spell names of animals.

#1 CUDK

#2 RFGO

#3 UEML

#4 TOTRE

Box of Clues

Stumped? Maybe you can find a clue below.

-Web-footed amphibian
-Fish-eating mammal related to the weasel
-Swimming bird
-Slow-moving reptile
-Horse/donkey combination
-Small rodent
-Large bird

#5 OUMES

#6 EUKTYR

Arrange the circled letters to solve the mystery answer.

MYSTERY ANSWER

BASEBALL

Unscramble the Jumbles, one letter
to each square, to spell words related
to baseball.

#1 BSAE

#2 ACHTC

#3 RRREO

Interesting
Baseball Facts

#4 NIGNIN

On June 28, 1910, the
Chicago Cubs' Joe Tinker
became the first major
league player to steal home
twice in one game.

#5 RSITEK

150 yards of wool yarn is
used to make one official
major league baseball.

#6 LRTIEP

Arrange the circled letters
to solve the mystery answer.

MYSTERY ANSWER

U.S. PRESIDENTS

JUMBLE BrainBusters! Junior

Unscramble the Jumbles, one letter to each square, to spell last names of U.S. presidents.

#1 ERAANG

#2 OHREOV

#3 LIOWNS

#4 TCILONN

#5 NONOJSH

#6 LCDOGIEO

PRESIDENTS OF THE
UNITED STATES OF AMERICA

1789-1797 George Washington	1889-1893 Benjamin Harrison
1797-1801 John Adams	1893-1897 Grover Cleveland
1801-1809 Thomas Jefferson	1897-1901 William McKinley
1809-1817 James Madison	1901-1909 Theodore (Teddy) Roosevelt
1817-1825 James Monroe	1909-1913 William Howard Taft
1825-1829 John Quincy Adams	1913-1921 Thomas Woodrow Wilson
1829-1837 Andrew Jackson	1921-1923 Warren G. Harding
1837-1841 Martin Van Buren	1923-1929 John Calvin Coolidge
1841 William Henry Harrison	1929-1933 Herbert Hoover
1841-1845 John Tyler	1933-1945 Franklin D. Roosevelt
1845-1849 James Polk	1945-1953 Harry S. Truman
1849-1850 Zachary Taylor	1953-1961 Dwight David Eisenhower
1850-1853 Millard Fillmore	1961-1963 John Fitzgerald Kennedy
1853-1857 Franklin Pierce	1963-1969 Lyndon B. Johnson
1857-1861 James Buchanan	1969-1974 Richard M. Nixon
1861-1865 Abraham Lincoln	1974-1977 Gerald R. Ford
1865-1869 Andrew Johnson	1977-1981 James (Jimmy) Carter
1869-1877 Ulysses S. Grant	1981-1989 Ronald Reagan
1877-1881 Rutherford B. Hayes	1989-1993 George W. Bush
1881 James A. Garfield	1993-2001 William Jefferson Clinton
1881-1885 Chester A. Arthur	2001- George Walker Bush
1885-1889 Stephen Grover Cleveland	

Arrange the circled letters to solve the mystery answer.

MYSTERY ANSWER

AROUND THE HOME

Unscramble the Jumbles, one letter to each square, to spell words related to things found around the home.

#1 HCIRA

#2 BCIKR

#3 HPOEN

Box of Clues

Stumped? Maybe you can find a clue below.

- Room bottom
- Electrical _____
- Seat for one person
- Car area
- Room top
- Communication device
- Building block

#4 FOLRO

#5 OTELTU

#6 RGAAEG

Arrange the circled letters to solve the mystery answer.

MYSTERY ANSWER

ELEMENTS

JUMBLE BrainBusters! Junior

Unscramble the Jumbles, one letter to each square, to spell names of elements.

#1 ODGL

#2 ENXNO

#3 ARIMUD

#4 LHEIMU

#5 SICINOL

Arrange the circled letters to solve the mystery answer.

MYSTERY ANSWER

Name	Gold	Potassium
Actinium	Hafnium	Praseodymium
Aluminum	Hassium	Promethium
Americium	Helium	Protactinium
Antimony	Holmium	Radium
Argon	Hydrogen	Radon
Arsenic	Indium	Rhenium
Astatine	Iodine	Rhodium
Barium	Iridium	Rubidium
Berkelium	Iron	Ruthenium
Beryllium	Krypton	Rutherfordium
Bismuth	Lanthanum	Samarium
Bohrium	Lawrencium	Scandium
Boron	Lead	Seaborgium
Bromine	Lithium	Selenium
Cadmium	Lutetium	Silicon
Calcium	Magnesium	Silver
Californium	Manganese	Sodium
Carbon	Meitnerium	Strontium
Cerium	Mendelevium	Sulfur
Cesium	Mercury	Tantalum
Chlorine	Molybdenum	Technetium
Chromium	Neodymium	Tellurium
Cobalt	Neon	Terbium
Copper	Neptunium	Thallium
Curium	Nickel	Thorium
Dubnium	Niobium	Thulium
Dysprosium	Nitrogen	Tin
Einsteinium	Nobelium	Titanium
Erbium	Osmium	Tungsten
Europium	Oxygen	Uranium
Fermium	Palladium	Vanadium
Fluorine	Phosphorus	Xenon
Francium	Platinum	Ytterbium
Gadolinium	Plutonium	Yttrium
Gallium	Polonium	Zinc
Germanium	Potassium	Zirconium

MAMMALS

Unscramble the Jumbles, one letter to each square, to spell names of mammals.

#1 ETRIG

#2 HRION

#3 LAEMC

#4 RAEEVB

#5 OABBON

#6 RAWUSL

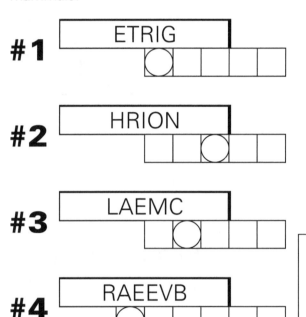

Box of Clues

Stumped? Maybe you can find a clue below.

- Dam builder
- Large ape with a dog-like muzzle
- Large, thick-skinned, three-toed plant eater
- Powerful cat
- Desert cargo carrier
- Common, burrowing animal
- Tusked, seal relative

Arrange the circled letters to solve the mystery answer.

MYSTERY ANSWER

STARTS WITH "L"

Unscramble the Jumbles, one letter to each square, to spell words that start with "L".

#1 GILHT

#2 KLCYU

#3 OLBYB

#4 SLENOS

#5 WALEYR

#6 NRLATNE

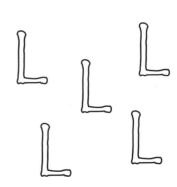

Box of Clues

Stumped? Maybe you can find a clue below.

- Attorney
- Reasonable, rational
- Fortunate
- Light source
- Entrance hall
- Exercise, assignment
- Sun output

Arrange the circled letters to solve the mystery answer.

MYSTERY ANSWER

BIRDS

Unscramble the Jumbles, one letter to each square, to spell types of birds.

#1 RCWO

#2 AEEGL

#3 TSOKR

#4 CNHIEKC

#5 EIUPNGN

#6 UTUVREL

Box of Clues

Stumped? Maybe you can find a clue below.

- Circling bird of prey
- Southern bird
- Bald _____
- Common farm bird
- Bird with colorful tail feathers
- Glassy black bird
- Wading bird with a long bill

Arrange the circled letters to solve the mystery answer.

MYSTERY ANSWER

SPORTS

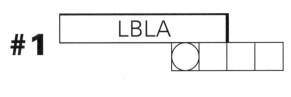

Unscramble the Jumbles, one letter to each square, to spell words related to sports.

#1 LBLA

#2 DKNU

#3 UKPC

#4 LGOEV

#5 RERRO

#6 ESOANS

Interesting Sports Facts

The first basketball rule book was published in the late 1800s.

The New York Yankees were the first team to travel to a game in an airplane.

Arrange the circled letters to solve the mystery answer.

MYSTERY ANSWER

U.S. STATES

JUMBLE BrainBusters! Junior

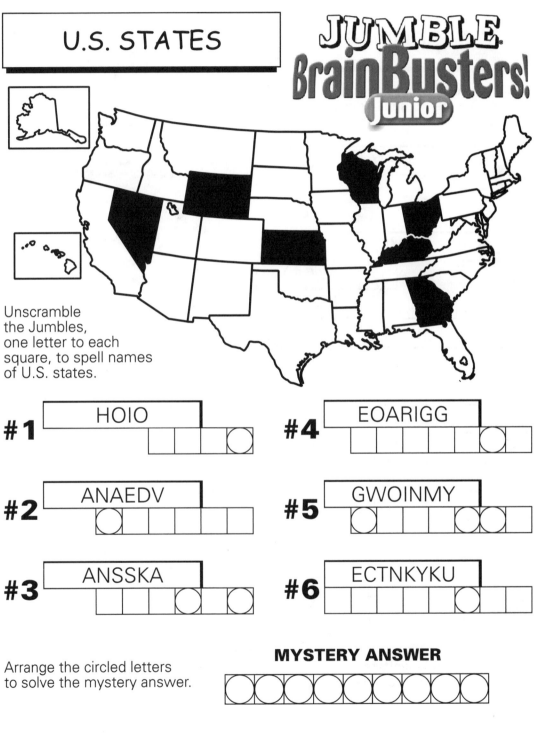

Unscramble the Jumbles, one letter to each square, to spell names of U.S. states.

#1 HOIO

#2 ANAEDV

#3 ANSSKA

#4 EOARIGG

#5 GWOINMY

#6 ECTNKYKU

Arrange the circled letters to solve the mystery answer.

MYSTERY ANSWER

SCHOOL

JUMBLE BrainBusters! Junior

Unscramble the Jumbles, one letter to each square, to spell words related to school.

#1 TMHA

#2 RAYDT

#3 EPILCN

#4 CLROEK

#5 WNSARE

#6 CISEENC

Box of Clues

Stumped? Maybe you can find a clue below.

-Storage compartment
-Writing instrument
-Chemistry, for example
-Late
-Algebra, for example
-Completion document
-Question's response

Arrange the circled letters to solve the mystery answer.

MYSTERY ANSWER

STARTS WITH A VOWEL

Unscramble the Jumbles, one letter to each square, to spell words that start with vowels (a,e,i,o,u).

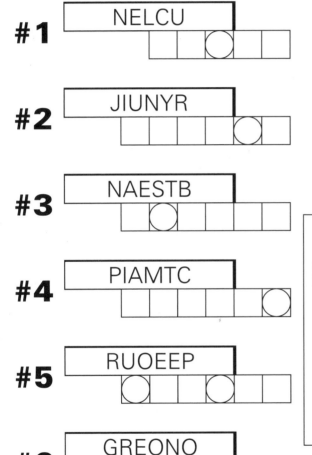

#1 NELCU

#2 JIUNYR

#3 NAESTB

#4 PIAMTC

#5 RUOEEP

#6 GREONO

Box of Clues

Stumped? Maybe you can find a clue below.

-Forcefully make contact
-"10"
-Damage, affliction
-A U.S. state
-Second-smallest continent
-Missing
-Male relative

Arrange the circled letters to solve the mystery answer.

MYSTERY ANSWER

ALL ABOUT MUSIC

Unscramble the Jumbles, one letter to each square, to spell words related to music.

#1 OIPNA

#2 COHDR

#3 METOP

Box of Clues

Stumped? Maybe you can find a clue below.

-Three or more tones played at the same time
-Pleasing musical arrangement
-Rate of speed
-Combination of notes or sounds
-Large instrument
-Flow of sound in music

#4 DEMYOL

#5 TYRHMH

Arrange the circled letters to solve the mystery answer.

MYSTERY ANSWER

STARTS WITH "M"

Unscramble the Jumbles, one letter to each square, to spell words that start with "M".

#1  XMIDE

#2 MEINA

#3  GAICM

#4  MUHTO

#5  TMIENT

#6  OIOMNT

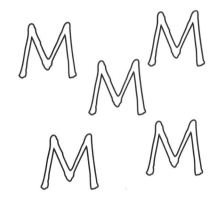

Box of Clues

Stumped? Maybe you can find a clue below.

-Movement
-Hand covering
-Combined
-Apparatus, device
-Tongue's home
-_____ trick
-A U.S. state

Arrange the circled letters to solve the mystery answer.

MYSTERY ANSWER

FAMOUS ATHLETES

Unscramble the Jumbles, one letter to each square, to spell last names of famous athletes.

#1 AGFR

#2 BCBO

#3 ARNAO

#4 YAPONT

#5 ROANJD

Box of Clues

Stumped? Maybe you can find a clue below.

-Home run hitter
-Michael _____
-Female tennis player
-Joe _____ (football player)
-Walter _____ (football player)
-Popular Jets quarterback
-Ty _____

#6 AANTHM

Arrange the circled letters to solve the mystery answer.

MYSTERY ANSWER

COUNTRIES

Unscramble the Jumbles, one letter to each square, to spell names of countries.

#1 UACB

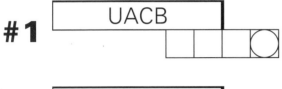

#2 YETPG

#3 NRFECA

#4 REEECG

#5 DSENEW

#6 EVINMAT

Box of Clues

Stumped? Maybe you can find a clue below.

-Scandinavian country
-Home to the Nile
-Home to Paris
-Home to Berlin
-Island country
-Home to Athens
-Asian country, home to Ho Chi Minh City

Arrange the circled letters to solve the mystery answer.

MYSTERY ANSWER

MAKING MOVIES

Unscramble the Jumbles, one letter to each square, to spell words related to making movies.

#1 RPPO

#2 NTSTU

#3 RCSITP

Box of Clues

Stumped? Maybe you can find a clue below.

-Starts with "S"; ends with "O"

-Starts with "C"; ends with "E"

-Starts with "C"; ends with "A"

-Starts with "S"; ends with "T"

-Starts with "S"; ends with "T"

-Starts with "W"; ends with "R"

-Starts with "P"; ends with "P"

#4 TUSIOD

#5 TWIRRE

#6 MACEAR

Arrange the circled letters to solve the mystery answer.

MYSTERY ANSWER

PLANET EARTH

Unscramble the Jumbles, one letter to each square, to spell words related to planet Earth.

#1 VRIRE

#2 USCTR

#3 ATREW

#4 LIADSN

Box of Clues

Stumped? Maybe you can find a clue below.

-Starts with "I"; ends with "D"

-Starts with "W"; ends with "R"

-Starts with "C"; ends with "T"

-Starts with "J"; ends with "E"

-Starts with "C"; ends with "T"

-Starts with "V"; ends with "O"

-Starts with "R"; ends with "R"

#5 NULJEG

#6 CVOALON

Arrange the circled letters to solve the mystery answer.

MYSTERY ANSWER

FOOTBALL

Unscramble the Jumbles, one letter to each square, to spell words related to football.

#1 ODNW

#2 TACHC

#3 CBOLK

#4 CTAELK

#5 MFLEBU

#6 TOIPOINS

Box of Clues

Stumped? Maybe you can find a clue below.

-Bring down
-Receive
-Quarterback, for example
-Mistake
-Offensive goal
-Offensive attempt
-Push away

Arrange the circled letters to solve the mystery answer.

MYSTERY ANSWER

U.S. PRESIDENTS

Unscramble the Jumbles, one letter to each square, to spell last names of U.S. presidents.

#1 LTREY

#2 AMSAD

#3 LISNOW

#4 SJCANOK

#5 FRIAGEDL

#6 HACANNUB

PRESIDENTS OF THE UNITED STATES OF AMERICA

1789-1797 George Washington
1797-1801 John Adams
1801-1809 Thomas Jefferson
1809-1817 James Madison
1817-1825 James Monroe
1825-1829 John Quincy Adams
1829-1837 Andrew Jackson
1837-1841 Martin Van Buren
1841 William Henry Harrison
1841-1845 John Tyler
1845-1849 James Polk
1849-1850 Zachary Taylor
1850-1853 Millard Fillmore
1853-1857 Franklin Pierce
1857-1861 James Buchanan
1861-1865 Abraham Lincoln
1865-1869 Andrew Johnson
1869-1877 Ulysses S. Grant
1877-1881 Rutherford B. Hayes
1881 James A. Garfield
1881-1885 Chester A. Arthur
1885-1889 Stephen Grover Cleveland

1889-1893 Benjamin Harrison
1893-1897 Grover Cleveland
1897-1901 William McKinley
1901-1909 Theodore (Teddy) Roosevelt
1909-1913 William Howard Taft
1913-1921 Thomas Woodrow Wilson
1921-1923 Warren G. Harding
1923-1929 John Calvin Coolidge
1929-1933 Herbert Hoover
1933-1945 Franklin D. Roosevelt
1945-1953 Harry S. Truman
1953-1961 Dwight David Eisenhower
1961-1963 John Fitzgerald Kennedy
1963-1969 Lyndon B. Johnson
1969-1974 Richard M. Nixon
1974-1977 Gerald R. Ford
1977-1981 James (Jimmy) Carter
1981-1989 Ronald Reagan
1989-1993 George W. Bush
1993-2001 William Jefferson Clinton
2001- George Walker Bush

Arrange the circled letters to solve the mystery answer.

MYSTERY ANSWER

ANIMALS

Unscramble the Jumbles, one letter to each square, to spell names of animals.

#1 AEEGL

#2 SEPEH

#3 NPAAD

#4 AIZDLR

#5 LTEUTR

#6 YNMEKO

Arrange the circled letters to solve the mystery answer.

MYSTERY ANSWER

FAMOUS PEOPLE

Unscramble the Jumbles, one letter to each square, to spell last names of famous people.

#1 NLGEN

#2 BOCYS

#3 SDIEYN

Box of Clues

Stumped? Maybe you can find a clue below.

-Funny Bill
-Entertaining Walt
-Actress Julia
-Singer, actor (1935-1977)
-John _____ (1940-1980)
-Astronaut John
-Colin _____

#4 NELNON

#5 OLPLEW

#6 TORBESR

Arrange the circled letters to solve the mystery answer.

MYSTERY ANSWER

WEATHER

Unscramble the Jumbles, one letter to each square, to spell words related to weather.

#1 ONSW

#2 LKEFA

#3 UIDHM

#4 REZEEB

#5 LUYCOD

#6 WTIERST

Box of Clues

Stumped? Maybe you can find a clue below.

-Starts with "T"; ends with "R"
-Starts with "F"; ends with "E"
-Starts with "H"; ends with "D"
-Starts with "S"; ends with "W"
-Starts with "T"; ends with "R"
-Starts with "B"; ends with "E"
-Starts with "C"; ends with "Y"

Arrange the circled letters to solve the mystery answer.

MYSTERY ANSWER

MATH

JUMBLE BrainBusters! Junior

Unscramble the Jumbled
letters, one letter to each square,
so that each equation is correct.

For example:
NONTEOEOW
O N E + O N E = T W O

#1 ROEFTHNEOEUR

☐☐☐☐ + ☐☐◯☐☐ = ☐☐◯☐

#2 ENHINNOEEITG

☐◯☐☐ − ☐◯☐☐ = ☐☐◯◯☐

#3 ZFVIEIEEROVF

☐☐☐☐☐ − ☐◯☐☐☐ = ☐☐◯☐

#4 TEESNIVFWEVO

☐☐☐☐☐☐☐ − ☐◯☐☐☐ = ☐☐◯☐

#5 ETOVUHRFRSEENE

☐☐◯☐☐ + ☐◯☐☐☐☐ = ☐☐☐◯☐☐

Arrange the circled letters
to solve the mystery equation.

MYSTERY EQUATION

◯◯◯◯◯ + ◯◯◯◯◯ = ◯◯◯◯◯◯

ELEMENTS

Unscramble the Jumbles, one letter to each square, to spell names of elements.

#1 ULFSRU

#2 POPCRE

#3 LHEIMU

#4 STUGENNT

#5 RHDOYGNE

Arrange the circled letters to solve the mystery answer.

MYSTERY ANSWER

Name	Gold	Potassium
Actinium	Hafnium	Praseodymium
Aluminum	Hassium	Promethium
Americium	Helium	Protactinium
Antimony	Holmium	Radium
Argon	Hydrogen	Radon
Arsenic	Indium	Rhenium
Astatine	Iodine	Rhodium
Barium	Iridium	Rubidium
Berkelium	Iron	Ruthenium
Beryllium	Krypton	Rutherfordium
Bismuth	Lanthanum	Samarium
Bohrium	Lawrencium	Scandium
Boron	Lead	Seaborgium
Bromine	Lithium	Selenium
Cadmium	Lutetium	Silicon
Calcium	Magnesium	Silver
Californium	Manganese	Sodium
Carbon	Meitnerium	Strontium
Cerium	Mendelevium	Sulfur
Cesium	Mercury	Tantalum
Chlorine	Molybdenum	Technetium
Chromium	Neodymium	Tellurium
Cobalt	Neon	Terbium
Copper	Neptunium	Thallium
Curium	Nickel	Thorium
Dubnium	Niobium	Thulium
Dysprosium	Nitrogen	Tin
Einsteinium	Nobelium	Titanium
Erbium	Osmium	Tungsten
Europium	Oxygen	Uranium
Fermium	Palladium	Vanadium
Fluorine	Phosphorus	Xenon
Francium	Platinum	Ytterbium
Gadolinium	Plutonium	Yttrium
Gallium	Polonium	Zinc
Germanium	Potassium	Zirconium

ADJECTIVES

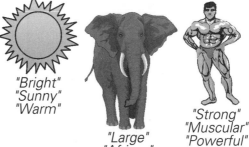

Unscramble the Jumbles, one letter to each square, to spell adjectives.

#1 UHEG
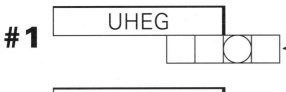

#2 SMIL

#3 CYUKL

#4 UNYFN

#5 AYHPP

#6 SRHFE

Arrange the circled letters to solve the mystery answer.

MYSTERY ANSWER

"Bright"
"Sunny"
"Warm"

"Large"
"African"
"Asian"

"Strong"
"Muscular"
"Powerful"

An adjective is a word that modifies a noun by describing it. An adjective might indicate a noun's quantity or extent, or specify a thing as distinct from something else.

Box of Clues

Stumped? Maybe you can find a clue below.

-Describe vegetables that have just been picked
-Describe a lottery winner
-Describe a thin person
-Describe a comedian
-Describe someone who is not in a good mood
-Describe someone who is in a good mood
-Describe Jupiter

OUTER SPACE

Unscramble the Jumbles, one letter to each square, to spell words related to outer space.

#1 XLYAAG

#2 SEMTYS

#3 UJIRTPE

#4 PNEUENT

Box of Clues

Stumped? Maybe you can find a clue below.

-Space rock
-The Milky Way, for example
-Closest planet to the sun
-"Great Red Spot's" home
-Uranus' outer neighbor
-Home to Titan (large moon)
-Solar _____

#5 RCMEYUR

#6 TASEIDOR

Arrange the circled letters to solve the mystery answer.

MYSTERY ANSWER

state

capitals

animals

JUMBLE®

BrainBusters

Junior

INTERMEDIATE
PUZZLES

human

body

outer

space

money

sports

STARTS WITH "P"

Unscramble the Jumbles, one letter to each square, to spell words that start with "P".

#1 PCNUH

#2 ONUPD

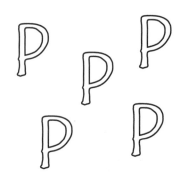

#3 CPIEDK

Box of Clues

Stumped? Maybe you can find a clue below.

-Weight unit
-Chosen
-Flat food
-_____ eye
-Manipulated figure
-Hit
-Rested

#4 APUESD

#5 EPPUTP

#6 TRPIAEV

Arrange the circled letters to solve the mystery answer.

MYSTERY ANSWER

THE HUMAN BODY

Unscramble the Jumbles, one letter to each square, to spell words related to the human body.

#1 UGLN

#2 JTINO

#3 RINBA

#4 TRAHTO

#5 NEAELM

#6 DERRMUA

Box of Clues

Stumped? Maybe you can find a clue below.

-Part of the neck
-Control center
-Breathing organ
-Wrist or ankle
-Sensitive mouth part
-Tooth covering
-Thin membrane that carries sound waves

Arrange the circled letters to solve the mystery answer.

MYSTERY ANSWER

MEANS THE OPPOSITE

JUMBLE BrainBusters! Junior

Unscramble the Jumbles, one letter to each square, to spell pairs of words with opposite meanings.

For example:

EIDW — NOAWRR
W I D E — N A R R O W

#1 ASEF — KRIYS

#2 LPSU — UMSIN

#3 LMIS — CTIKH

#4 RGWO — RNISHK

#5 HEREC — OGOML

Arrange the circled letters to solve the mystery answer.

MYSTERY ANSWER

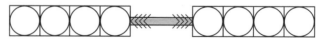

LARGE CITIES

Unscramble the Jumbles, one letter to each square, to spell names of large cities.

#1 LSINOB

#2 REBINL

#3 NLOOND

#4 DSYEYN

#5 OMCOSW

#6 ACIGCOH

Box of Clues

Stumped? Maybe you can find a clue below.

-Largest city in Russia
-Largest city in Portugal
-Large U.S. Midwestern city
-Large Australian city
-Largest city in Spain
-Largest city in Germany
-Largest city in England

Arrange the circled letters to solve the mystery answer.

MYSTERY ANSWER

RHYMES

JUMBLE
BrainBusters!
Junior

Unscramble the Jumbles, one letter to each square, to spell pairs of rhyming words.

For example:

| LBPIM | MIPCH |
| B L I M P | C H I M P |

#1 ABDN   NDHA

#2 UOPDN   ORNUD

#3 OSEOL   ONSEO

#4 ELEDG   DGEWE

#5 TEERLT   RTEEBT

Arrange the circled letters to solve the mystery answer.

MYSTERY ANSWER

TIME LINE

JUMBLE BrainBusters! Junior

Unscramble the Jumbles, one letter to each square, to spell words as suggested by the time line.

#1 **1798** Napoleon Bonaparte invades _____

#2 **1832** First _____ built in the U.S.

#3 **1846** _____ machine invented

#4 **1912** S.S. Titanic sinks in the _____

#5 **1986** Hole discovered in the _____ layer

#6 **1989** Emperor Hirohito dies in _____

#1 GEYTP

#2 LRIAYWA

#3 ESIGWN

#4 NALTAICT

#5 ZOOEN

#6 PAJNA

Arrange the circled letters to solve the mystery answer.

MYSTERY ANSWER

1892 The _____ is invented

SPORTS TEAMS

Unscramble the Jumbles, one letter to each square, to spell names of professional sports teams.

#1 GKNIS

#2 ULBSL

#3 XEOSP

#4 GIMAC

#5 AGINST

#6 BOCYWOS

Box of Clues

Stumped? Maybe you can find a clue below.

- -Canadian baseball team
- -New York _____ or San Francisco _____
- -Orlando _____
- -Texas football team
- -The Boston _____
- -Sacramento basketball team
- -M.J.'s old team

Arrange the circled letters to solve the mystery answer.

MYSTERY ANSWER

BIRDS

JUMBLE
BrainBusters!
Junior

Unscramble the Jumbles, one letter
to each square, to spell types of birds.

#1 ODEV

#2 AHKW

#3 LAEEG

#4 GPIONE

#5 KRUTYE

#6 ROTSCIH

Box of Clues

Stumped? Maybe you can find a clue
below.

-Starts with "P"; ends with "N"
-Starts with "D"; ends with "E"
-Starts with "T"; ends with "Y"
-Starts with "C"; ends with "L"
-Starts with "H"; ends with "K"
-Starts with "E"; ends with "E"
-Starts with "O"; ends with "H"

Arrange the circled letters
to solve the mystery answer.

MYSTERY ANSWER

OCCUPATIONS

Unscramble the Jumbles, one letter
to each square, to spell occupations.

#1 TIPLO

#2 HUTARO

#3 RAERBB

#4 ODTCRO

#5 TANJIRO

#6 MLUPERB

Arrange the circled letters
to solve the mystery answer.

Box of Clues

Stumped? Maybe you can find a clue
below.

-Starts with "D"; ends with "R"
-Starts with "J"; ends with "R"
-Starts with "A"; ends with "R"
-Starts with "R"; ends with "R"
-Starts with "B"; ends with "R"
-Starts with "P"; ends with "R"
-Starts with "P"; ends with "T"

MYSTERY ANSWER

EUROPEAN COUNTRIES

Unscramble the Jumbles, one letter to each square, to spell names of European countries.

#1  CEEERG

#2  NOLDPA

#3  SARIUAT

#4  GENNDAL

#5  GUHYANR

#6  RNEAKDM

Box of Clues

Stumped? Maybe you can find a clue below.

-Home to Warsaw (starts with "P")
-Home to London (starts with "E")
-Home to Athens (starts with "G")
-Home to Berlin (starts with "G")
-Home to Vienna (starts with "A")
-Home to Copenhagen (starts with "D")
-Home to Budapest (starts with "H")

Arrange the circled letters to solve the mystery answer.

MYSTERY ANSWER

ELEMENTS

JUMBLE
BrainBusters!
Junior

Unscramble
the Jumbles, one letter to
each square, to spell names
of elements.

| H | — Atomic # |
| | — Atomic Symbol |

THE PERIODIC TABLE

1 H																		2 He ★
3 Li	4 Be											5 B ★	6 C	7 N	8 O ★	9 F	10 Ne
11 Na	12 Mg											13 Al	14 Si	15 P	16 S	17 Cl	18 Ar
19 K	20 Ca	21 Sc	22 Ti	23 V	24 Cr	25 Mn	26 Fe ★	27 Co	28 Ni	29 Cu ★	30 Zn ★	31 Ga	32 Ge	33 As	34 Se	35 Br	36 Kr
37 Rb	38 Sr	39 Y	40 Zr	41 Nb	42 Mo	43 Tc	44 Ru	45 Rh	46 Pd	47 Ag	48 Cd	49 In	50 Sn	51 Sb	52 Te	53 I	54 Xe
55 Cs	56 Ba	57-71 Lathanide series (rare earth elements)	72 Hf	73 Ta	74 W	75 Re	76 Os	77 Ir	78 Pt	79 Au	80 Hg ★	81 Tl	82 Pb	83 Bi	84 Po	85 At	86 Rn
87 Fr	88 Ra	89-103 Actinide series (radioactive rare earth elements)	104 Unq	105 Unp	106 Unh	107 Uns		108 Une									

#1 ZCIN

#2 OINR

#3 RONBO

#4 GEONXY

#5 POECRP

#6 LHIMUE

Arrange the circled letters
to solve the mystery answer.

MYSTERY ANSWER

NOUNS

Unscramble the Jumbles, one letter to each square, to spell nouns.

"Animal"
"Dinosaur"
"Reptile"

"Runner"
"Athlete"
"Racer"

"Tree"
"Plant"
"Cypress"

A noun is a word that is the name of something (as in a person, animal, place, thing, quality, idea or action).

#1 EIHV

#2 AFMR

#3 UADTL

#4 PAELP

#5 NFEEC

#6 SLGSA

Box of Clues

Stumped? Maybe you can find a clue below.

-Grown-up
-Land devoted to agriculture
-Barricade, barrier
-Type of fruit
-Bees' collective home
-Means of transportation
-Window material

Arrange the circled letters to solve the mystery answer.

MYSTERY ANSWER

STARTS WITH "S"

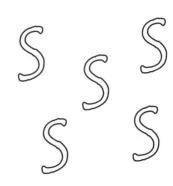

Unscramble the Jumbles, one letter to each square, to spell words that start with "S".

#1 STIGH

#2 DSUEND

#3 GSOPEN

#4 SLETAET

#5 CSUPSTE

#6 RCSATET

Arrange the circled letters to solve the mystery answer.

Box of Clues

Stumped? Maybe you can find a clue below.

-A U.S. city
-Happen quickly
-Vision
-Daily ending
-Person believed to be guilty
-Spread
-Porous creature

MYSTERY ANSWER

WEATHER

Unscramble the Jumbles, one letter to each square, to spell words related to weather.

#1 ARIF

#2 DWIN

#3 NOFTR

Box of Clues

Stumped? Maybe you can find a clue below.

-Cold or warm _____
-Not stormy or cloudy
-Colorful phenomenon
-Weather disturbance
-Destructive hurricane product
-Gentle wind
-Tornado nickname

#4 TSMOR

#5 ZEEEBR

#6 STEWRIT

Arrange the circled letters to solve the mystery answer.

MYSTERY ANSWER

U.S. STATES

Unscramble the Jumbles, one letter to each square, to spell names of U.S. states.

#1 LODFAIR

#2 EOIGARG

#3 NYOWIGM

#4 TNONAAM

#5 MENOTRV

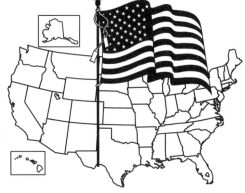

Box of Clues

Stumped? Maybe you can find a clue below.

-Starts with "G"; ends with "A"
-Starts with "M"; ends with "A"
-Starts with "F"; ends with "A"
-Starts with "D"; ends with "E"
-Starts with "V"; ends with "T"
-Starts with "W"; ends with "G"

Arrange the circled letters to solve the mystery answer.

MYSTERY ANSWER

SPORTS

JUMBLE
BrainBusters!
Junior

Unscramble the Jumbles, one letter to each square, to spell words related to sports.

#1 RKIN

#2 RISEKT

#3 OROIEK

#4 FEEDTA

#5 LFUEBM

#6 HPIERTC

Box of Clues

Stumped? Maybe you can find a clue below.

- Pedro Martinez's position
- Beginner
- Offense's opponent
- Football mistake
- Ice hockey playing area
- Beat or loss
- Pitcher's goal

Arrange the circled letters to solve the mystery answer.

MYSTERY ANSWER

MAMMALS

Unscramble the Jumbles, one letter to each square, to spell names of mammals.

#1 UKSKN

#2 HSEPE

#3 HCIPM

#4 BARITB

#5 EHEAHTC

#6 COACONR

Box of Clues

Stumped? Maybe you can find a clue below.

-"Masked" tree climber
-Cud-chewing, goat relative
-Fast cat
-Black and white animal
-Type of ape
-Large rodent with stiff hair
-Long-eared, short-tailed mammal

Arrange the circled letters to solve the mystery answer.

MYSTERY ANSWER

COUNTRIES

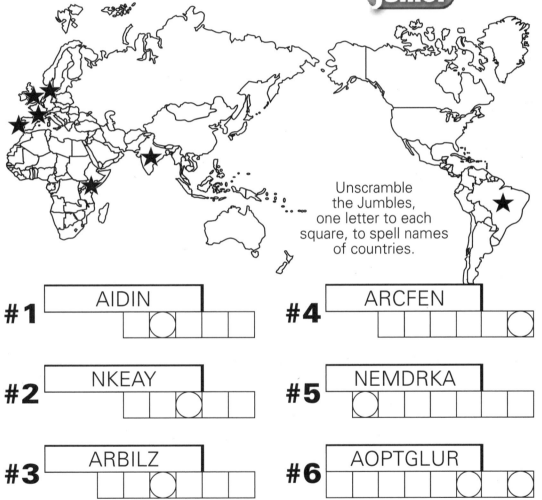

JUMBLE BrainBusters! Junior

Unscramble the Jumbles, one letter to each square, to spell names of countries.

#1 AIDIN

#2 NKEAY

#3 ARBILZ

#4 ARCFEN

#5 NEMDRKA

#6 AOPTGLUR

Arrange the circled letters to solve the mystery answer.

MYSTERY ANSWER

CLOTHING

JUMBLE BrainBusters! Junior

Unscramble the Jumbles, one letter to each square, to spell words related to clothing.

#1 SCOK

#2 RIHTS

#3 SEDRS

Box of Clues

Stumped? Maybe you can find a clue below.

-Starts with "D"; ends with "S"
-Starts with "B"; ends with "N"
-Starts with "M"; ends with "N"
-Starts with "U"; ends with "M"
-Starts with "S"; ends with "K"
-Starts with "S"; ends with "T"
-Starts with "F"; ends with "C"

#4 AFRICB

#5 TBOUNT

#6 NTEITM

Arrange the circled letters to solve the mystery answer.

MYSTERY ANSWER

U.S. STATE CAPITALS

Unscramble the Jumbles, one letter to each square, to spell U.S. state capitals.

#1  TOSNBO

#2  EHNIXOP

#3  CBKIRSMA

#4  BOCIAMUL

#5  TRHODRFA

Arrange the circled letters to solve the mystery answer.

Montgomery	Baton Rouge	Columbus
Juneau	Augusta	Oklahoma City
Phoenix	Annapolis	Salem
Little Rock	Boston	Harrisburg
Sacramento	Lansing	Providence
Denver	St. Paul	Columbia
Hartford	Jackson	Pierre
Dover	Jefferson City	Nashville
Tallahassee	Helena	Austin
Atlanta	Lincoln	Salt Lake City
Honolulu	Carson City	Montpelier
Boise	Concord	Richmond
Springfield	Trenton	Olympia
Indianapolis	Santa Fe	Charleston
Des Moines	Albany	Madison
Topeka	Raleigh	Cheyenne
Frankfort	Bismarck	

MYSTERY ANSWER

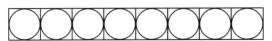

Box of Clues

Stumped? Maybe you can find a clue below.

- Arizona   -Virginia
- South Carolina   -Connecticut
- Massachusetts
- North Dakota

HERBIVORES

Unscramble the Jumbles, one letter to each square, to spell words herbivores.

#1 PHPIO

#2 LAMCE

#3 EZARB

#4 FAIREFG

Herbivore

Herbivore is the term commonly applied to any animal whose diet consists wholly or largely of plant material.

#5 FFAUOBL

#6 GRAKOOAN

Arrange the circled letters to solve the mystery answer.

MYSTERY ANSWER

ADJECTIVES

"Bright"
"Sunny"
"Warm"

"Large"
"African"
"Asian"

"Strong"
"Muscular"
"Powerful"

Unscramble the Jumbles, one letter
to each square, to spell adjectives.

#1 DKIN

#2 ADHR

#3 OGDO

#4 EHYVA

#5 OURHG

#6 NMIRO

An adjective is a word that modifies
a noun by describing it. An adjective
might indicate a noun's quantity or
extent, or specify a thing as distinct
from something else.

Arrange the circled letters
to solve the mystery answer.

MYSTERY ANSWER

Box of Clues

Stumped? Maybe you can find a clue
below.

-Solid, firm
-Small, insignificant
-Unwieldy, weighty
-Jagged, uneven
-Pleasant, favorable
-Aimless, purposeless
-Good-hearted, humane

OUTER SPACE

Unscramble the Jumbles, one letter to each square, to spell words related to outer space.

#1 LUPOT

#2 AAGYXL

#3 BULHEB

Box of Clues

Stumped? Maybe you can find a clue below.

-Large collection of stars
-The moon to Earth
-Home to Europa and Io
-_____ Space Telescope
-This planet was detected in 1781
-Ninth planet (on average)
-Moonless, rocky planet near the sun

#4 AUNSRU

#5 PITJREU

#6 ERURYCM

Arrange the circled letters to solve the mystery answer.

MYSTERY ANSWER

U.S. CITIES

JUMBLE BrainBusters! Junior

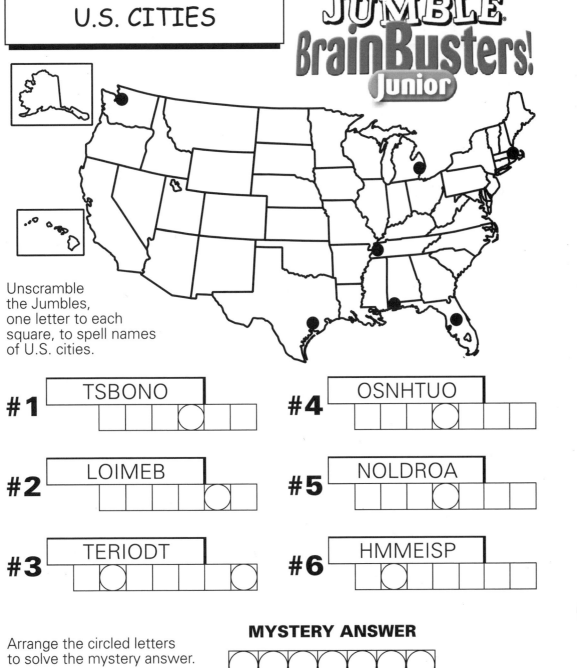

Unscramble the Jumbles, one letter to each square, to spell names of U.S. cities.

#1 TSBONO

#2 LOIMEB

#3 TERIODT

#4 OSNHTUO

#5 NOLDROA

#6 HMMEISP

Arrange the circled letters to solve the mystery answer.

MYSTERY ANSWER

ELEMENTS

Unscramble the Jumbles, one letter to each square, to spell names of elements.

#1  BCOATL

#2  OSDIMU

#3  RYPKTNO

#4  ERCMUYR

#5  LCOHRIEN

Arrange the circled letters to solve the mystery answer.

MYSTERY ANSWER

THE PERIODIC TABLE

Name	Gold	Potassium
Actinium	Hafnium	Praseodymium
Aluminum	Hassium	Promethium
Americium	Helium	Protactinium
Antimony	Holmium	Radium
Argon	Hydrogen	Radon
Arsenic	Indium	Rhenium
Astatine	Iodine	Rhodium
Barium	Iridium	Rubidium
Berkelium	Iron	Ruthenium
Beryllium	Krypton	Rutherfordium
Bismuth	Lanthanum	Samarium
Bohrium	Lawrencium	Scandium
Boron	Lead	Seaborgium
Bromine	Lithium	Selenium
Cadmium	Lutetium	Silicon
Calcium	Magnesium	Silver
Californium	Manganese	Sodium
Carbon	Meitnerium	Strontium
Cerium	Mendelevium	Sulfur
Cesium	Mercury	Tantalum
Chlorine	Molybdenum	Technetium
Chromium	Neodymium	Tellurium
Cobalt	Neon	Terbium
Copper	Neptunium	Thallium
Curium	Nickel	Thorium
Dubnium	Niobium	Thulium
Dysprosium	Nitrogen	Tin
Einsteinium	Nobelium	Titanium
Erbium	Osmium	Tungsten
Europium	Oxygen	Uranium
Fermium	Palladium	Vanadium
Fluorine	Phosphorus	Xenon
Francium	Platinum	Ytterbium
Gadolinium	Plutonium	Yttrium
Gallium	Polonium	Zinc
Germanium	Potassium	Zirconium

U.S. STATES

JUMBLE BrainBusters! Junior

Unscramble the Jumbles, one letter to each square, to spell names of U.S. states.

#1 AHIAIW

#2 NAASSK

#3 EOONGR

#4 LRIFADO

#5 ZAIORAN

#6 NERVOTM

Box of Clues

Stumped? Maybe you can find a clue below.

-Home to Disney World
-Home to Wichita and Topeka
-Island state
-Home to Portland
-Home to Tulsa
-New England state; home to Burlington
-Home to the Grand Canyon

Arrange the circled letters to solve the mystery answer.

MYSTERY ANSWER
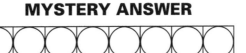

MATH

JUMBLE
BrainBusters!
Junior

Unscramble the Jumbled letters, one letter to each square, so that each equation is correct.

For example: NONTEOEOW
ONE + ONE = TWO

#1 ZIXSROXEIS

☐☐☐☐ + ☐☐◯☐☐ = ☐◯☐☐

#2 ZNNEEOOERO

☐◯☐ + ☐☐☐◯☐ = ☐◯☐☐

#3 VSIWSXLEEITX

☐◯☐☐ + ☐☐☐☐ = ◯☐☐☐☐☐

#4 ZEGIEHRHOTEITG

☐☐☐◯☐☐ − ☐◯☐☐☐ = ☐☐◯☐☐

#5 ESEENVUOREEVNLF

☐☐☐☐☐◯☐ + ☐☐☐☐☐ = ☐☐☐☐☐☐☐◯

Arrange the circled letters to solve the mystery equation.

MYSTERY EQUATION

◯◯◯◯ − ◯◯◯◯◯ = ◯◯◯

AUTOMOBILES

Unscramble the Jumbles, one letter to each square, to spell words related to automobiles.

#1 RTUKN

#2 GGAEU

#3 LAAMR

#4 GEINEN

#5 UBREPM

#6 HXSEUAT

Box of Clues

Stumped? Maybe you can find a clue below.

- Protective system
- Muffler's system
- Car storage area
- Front or rear protector
- Storage compartment
- Gas _____
- Power source

Arrange the circled letters to solve the mystery answer.

MYSTERY ANSWER

ALL ABOUT PLANTS

Unscramble the Jumbles, one letter to each square, to spell words related to plants.

#1 LAEAG

#2 RTKNU

#3 ROCIDH

#4 TCAUSC

#5 LFOREW

#6 MAOOBB

Arrange the circled letters to solve the mystery answer.

Box of Clues

Stumped? Maybe you can find a clue below.

-Starts with "C"; ends with "S"
-Starts with "A"; ends with "E"
-Starts with "B"; ends with "H"
-Starts with "O"; ends with "D"
-Starts with "F"; ends with "R"
-Starts with "T"; ends with "K"
-Starts with "B"; ends with "O"

MYSTERY ANSWER

ALL ABOUT MONEY

Unscramble the Jumbles, one letter to each square, to spell words related to money.

#1 LILB

#2 HCSA

#3 OLNA

#4 TEWLLA

#5 CREEITP

#6 TACNOUC

Box of Clues

Stumped? Maybe you can find a clue below.

-Checking _____
-Written record
-One dollar _____
-Money transporter
-Charge for borrowed money
-_____ register
-A mortgage, for example

Arrange the circled letters to solve the mystery answer.

MYSTERY ANSWER

FOOD

Unscramble the Jumbles, one letter to each square, to spell words related to food.

#1 KAEC

#2 PAELP

#3 CAKSN

#4 EHSCEE

#5 FWAELF

#6 UPNDIGD

Box of Clues

Stumped? Maybe you can find a clue below.

-Starts with "C"; ends with "E"
-Starts with "A"; ends with "E"
-Starts with "C"; ends with "E"
-Starts with "S"; ends with "K"
-Starts with "S"; ends with "H"
-Starts with "P"; ends with "G"
-Starts with "W"; ends with "E"

Arrange the circled letters to solve the mystery answer.

MYSTERY ANSWER

POETRY

Unscramble the Jumbles, one letter to each square, to spell words found in the poem.

#1 TEADEB

#2 VEANSEL

#3 GTIHM

#4 HFTIG

#5 MLJUEB

WORDS by Kim Nolan

Words can _____ #1
And words can agree
Some words _____ #2
While others set free

Some words are meek
Yet others have _____ #3
Some words resolve
While other words _____ #4

Some words have grace
While some words fumble
Some words stand straight
And some words _____ #5

Arrange the circled letters to solve the mystery answer. (The mystery answer is not in the poem.)

MYSTERY ANSWER

ANIMALS

Unscramble the Jumbles, one letter to each square, to spell names of animals.

#1 HIFS

#2 RBCA

#3 GTIRE

#4 KSUKN

#5 BRAITB

#6 OUCARG

Box of Clues

Stumped? Maybe you can find a clue below.

-Saber-toothed _____
-Fluffy, burrowing mammal
-A bass or tuna, for example
-Type of bird
-Black and white mammal
-Another name for puma
-Type of crustacean

Arrange the circled letters to solve the mystery answer.

MYSTERY ANSWER

MATH

JUMBLE BrainBusters! Junior

Unscramble the Jumbled
letters, one letter to each square,
so that each equation is correct.

For example: NONTEOEOW
ONE + ONE = TWO

#1 RNEEOZEOZOR

□□□□ × □□○□ = □□□○

#2 UOOEUFNRORF

□□□□ × □○□□ = ○□□○

#3 TETEYTNWNNTE

□□□□ + ○□□ = □○□□□□

#4 VENOSEEHIGETN

□□□□ + □□□○□ = □□□○□

#5 TSTYTIOXIRYWHT

□○□○□ ÷ □□□□ = □○□□□□

Arrange the circled letters
to solve the mystery equation.

MYSTERY EQUATION

○○○ × ○○○○ = ○○○○○

95

PUZZLE

94

RHYMES

Jumble BrainBusters! Junior

Unscramble the Jumbles, one letter to each square, to spell pairs of rhyming words.

For example:

LBPIM — MIPCH

B L I M P — C H I M P

#1 ATSY — APYR

#2 GEDEH — DGEEW

#3 ORWFN — OBNRW

#4 TPEKCO — KOLETC

#5 EBERTT — TWSAERE

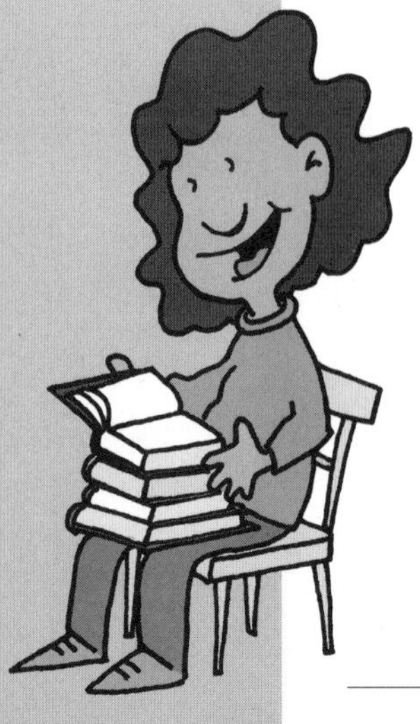

Arrange the circled letters to solve the mystery answer.

MYSTERY ANSWER

TIME LINE

Unscramble the Jumbles, one letter to each square, to spell words as suggested by the time line.

#1 1768 James Cook makes first voyage to the _____

#2 1841 British annex New _____

#3 1862 Gatling patents the _____ gun

#4 1920 _____ broadcasting begins

#5 1922 Mussolini assumes power in _____

#6 1980 John _____ dies

#1 AICPICF

#2 AELZNDA

#3 CMHIAEN

#4 ARIOD

#5 TILYA

#6 NELONN

Arrange the circled letters to solve the mystery answer.

1819 United States purchases _____

MYSTERY ANSWER

ELEMENTS

JUMBLE BrainBusters! Junior

Unscramble the Jumbles, one letter to each square, to spell names of elements.

#1 RNIO

#2 OGDL

#3 YOENGX

#4 POCERP

#5 LHIMUE

#6 DSMOIU

An element is a fundamental substance consisting of atoms of only one kind that cannot be broken down into simpler substances.

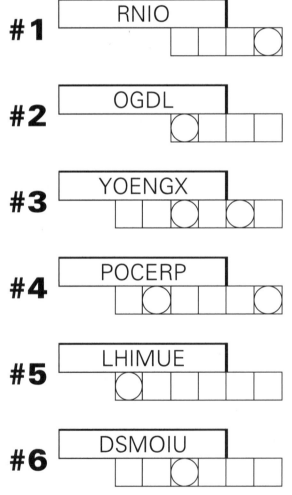

Box of Clues

Stumped? Maybe you can find a clue below.

-Starts with "G"; ends with "D"

-Starts with "C"; ends with "R"

-Starts with "H"; ends with "N"

-Starts with "I"; ends with "N"

-Starts with "O"; ends with "N"

-Starts with "S"; ends with "M"

-Starts with "H"; ends with "M"

Arrange the circled letters to solve the mystery answer.

MYSTERY ANSWER

U.S. STATE CAPITALS

Unscramble the Jumbles, one letter to each square, to spell U.S. state capitals.

#1 OIBES

#2 UTAINS

#3 UNJAUE

#4 KOTPAE

Box of Clues

Stumped? Maybe you can find a clue below.

-The capital of Texas
-The capital of Alaska
-The capital of Massachusetts
-The capital of Michigan
-The capital of Nebraska
-The capital of Kansas
-The capital of Idaho

#5 NLAINGS

#6 CLOILNN

Arrange the circled letters to solve the mystery answer.

MYSTERY ANSWER

WEATHER

Unscramble the Jumbles, one letter
to each square, to spell words related
to weather.

#1 APDM

#2 LFODO

#3 CCIEIL

#4 DEEERG

#5 HUETRND

#6 CFRAEOST

Arrange the circled letters
to solve the mystery answer.

Interesting Weather Facts

Stampede Pass, Wash.,
receives an average of more
than 400 inches of snow a
year. It is considered the
snowiest city in the United
States.

Lightning zips along at
90,000 miles a second.

MYSTERY ANSWER

LARGE CITIES

Unscramble the Jumbles, one letter to each square, to spell names of large cities.

#1 RAWSWA

#2 AESTLET

#3 OORTONT

#4 OHUSONT

Box of Clues

Stumped? Maybe you can find a clue below.

- -_____, U.S.A. (starts with "S")
- -_____, Scotland (starts with "G")
- -_____, Poland (starts with "W")
- -_____, Canada (starts with "T")
- -_____, U.S.A. (starts with "H")
- -_____, Canada (starts with "M")
- -_____, U.S.A. (starts with "L")

#5 GLSAOWG

#6 TONEMALR

Arrange the circled letters to solve the mystery answer.

MYSTERY ANSWER

PRESIDENTS' FIRST NAMES

Unscramble the Jumbles, one letter to each square, to spell first names of U.S. presidents.

#1 RHYRA

#2 EGGERO

#3 RREGOV

#4 TAINRM

#5 WIHDTG

#6 TBERHRE

Interesting Presidential Facts

The first woman to run for president of the United States was Victoria Woodhall. She ran in 1872.

Arnold Schwarzenegger bought President John F. Kennedy's golf clubs at an auction in 1996. He paid $772,500.

Arrange the circled letters to solve the mystery answer.

MYSTERY ANSWER

STARTS WITH "T"

Unscramble the Jumbles, one letter to each square, to spell words that start with "T".

#1  TCIHK

#2  TLATET

#3  DUTEOX

#4  RTOHYP

#5  ATIRFCF

#6  NTOTIHG

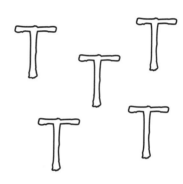

Box of Clues

Stumped? Maybe you can find a clue below.

- Formal suit
- Tell
- Dense, wide
- Prize
- Farm machine
- Later today
- Road congestion

Arrange the circled letters to solve the mystery answer.

MYSTERY ANSWER

COUNTRIES

Unscramble the Jumbles, one letter to each square, to spell names of countries.

#1 PJANA

#2 NORJAD

#3 DILFANN

Box of Clues

Stumped? Maybe you can find a clue below.

-Starts with "M"; ends with "O"

-Starts with "J"; ends with "N"

-Starts with "M"; ends with "A"

-Starts with "J"; ends with "N"

-Starts with "H"; ends with "Y"

-Starts with "F"; ends with "D"

-Starts with "B"; ends with "M"

#4 GEBIMUL

#5 NUHRYAG

#6 OCRCMOO

Arrange the circled letters to solve the mystery answer.

MYSTERY ANSWER

THE HUMAN BODY

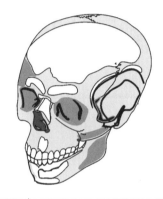

Unscramble the Jumbles, one letter to each square, to spell words related to the human body.

#1 RINBA

#2 HSTEC

#3 TOHTO

#4 MUHTO

#5 AREYRT

#6 NTOUEG

Box of Clues

Stumped? Maybe you can find a clue below.

-Starts with "A"; ends with "Y"
-Starts with "B"; ends with "N"
-Starts with "T"; ends with "H"
-Starts with "T"; ends with "E"
-Starts with "M"; ends with "H"
-Starts with "S"; ends with "H"
-Starts with "C"; ends with "T"

Arrange the circled letters to solve the mystery answer.

MYSTERY ANSWER

ABRAHAM LINCOLN

Unscramble the Jumbles, one letter to each square, to spell words related to Abraham Lincoln.

#1 AIRLP

#2 ACINB

#3 CSEHEP

#4 LWYARE

#5 ADBEET

#6 TKNUEKCY

Arrange the circled letters to solve the mystery answer.

Box of Clues

Stumped? Maybe you can find a clue below.

- Lincoln's birth state
- Lincoln-Douglas discussion
- Lincoln was born in one
- The Gettysburg Address, for example
- Lincoln title
- Month of Lincoln's death
- Lincoln left politics to become one in 1849

MYSTERY ANSWER

OCCUPATIONS

Unscramble the Jumbles, one letter to each square, to spell occupations.

#1 AOTIRL

#2 EUTBRL

#3 ROBERK

Box of Clues

Stumped? Maybe you can find a clue below.

-Starts with "B"; ends with "R"

-Starts with "S"; ends with "N"

-Starts with "T"; ends with "R"

-Starts with "B"; ends with "R"

-Starts with "J"; ends with "R"

-Starts with "W"; ends with "R"

-Starts with "C"; ends with "R"

#4 ARSHEIC

#5 UORSGNE

#6 REEWJEL

Arrange the circled letters to solve the mystery answer.

MYSTERY ANSWER

COUNTRY FLAGS

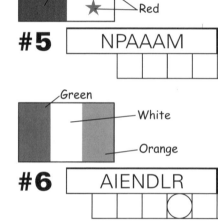

Unscramble the Jumbles, one letter to each square, to spell names of countries, as suggested by the flags.

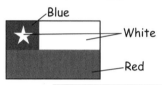

#1 HCIEL

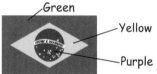

#2 RBIALZ

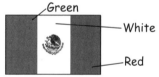

#3 EXIOCM

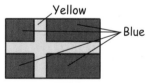

#4 WEENDS

#5 NPAAAM

#6 AIENDLR

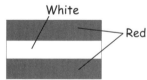

#7 RATIASU

Arrange the circled letters to solve the mystery answer.

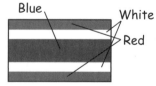

MYSTERY ANSWER

ADVERBS

Unscramble the Jumbles, one letter to each square, to spell adverbs.

#1 ERLEYF

#2 LGLYAD

#3 LOBYDL

#4 LOPOYR

#5 LACLYM

#6 LCEOSYL

"The runner ran quickly."
"The runner ran slowly."

An adverb is a word used to modify a verb, an adjective, another adverb, a preposition, a phrase, a clause or a sentence. It is often used to show degree, manner, place, or time.

Box of Clues

Stumped? Maybe you can find a clue below.

-Badly
-Without restrictions
-In an attentive manner
-Nearby; in the region of origin
-Bravely
-Smoothly, without getting upset
-Happily, with pleasure

Arrange the circled letters to solve the mystery answer.

MYSTERY ANSWER

OUTER SPACE

Unscramble the Jumbles, one letter to each square, to spell words related to outer space.

#1 TOIRB

#2 MOTEC

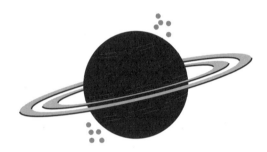

#3 OALOLP

#4 TSUNRA

Box of Clues

Stumped? Maybe you can find a clue below.

-NASA's moon landing mission
-Halley's _____
-_____ belt
-Planetary motion around the sun
-_____ Space Center
-Solar _____
-Jupiter's outer neighbor

#5 TSMESY

#6 ENYKNDE

Arrange the circled letters to solve the mystery answer.

MYSTERY ANSWER

ANIMALS

Unscramble the Jumbles, one letter to each square, to spell names of animals.

#1 ODEV

#2 UPAM

#3 NHYAE

#4 TORET

#5 HCIPM

#6 AECLM

Box of Clues

Stumped? Maybe you can find a clue below.

-Starts with "C"; ends with "P"
-Starts with "P"; ends with "A"
-Starts with "H"; ends with "A"
-Starts with "D"; ends with "E"
-Starts with "R"; ends with "N"
-Starts with "C"; ends with "L"
-Starts with "O"; ends with "R"

Arrange the circled letters to solve the mystery answer.

MYSTERY ANSWER

SCHOOL

JUMBLE BrainBusters! Junior

Unscramble the Jumbles, one letter to each square, to spell words related to school.

#1 STET

#2 NFKUL

#3 CLOERK

#4 RLIAYRB

#5 YSIORTH

#6 OECLELG

Box of Clues

Stumped? Maybe you can find a clue below.

-Quiet area
-Past's subject
-Fail
-Higher education
-Chemistry, for example
-Quiz
-Storage compartment

Arrange the circled letters to solve the mystery answer.

MYSTERY ANSWER

NOUNS

Unscramble the Jumbles, one letter
to each square, to spell nouns.

"Animal"
"Dinosaur"
"Reptile"

"Runner"
"Athlete"
"Racer"

"Tree"
"Plant"
"Cypress"

A noun is *a word that is the name
of something (as in a person, animal,
place, thing, quality, idea or action).*

#1 GLFA

#2 ANCIB

#3 RPPAE

#4 ENYPN

#5 BOHYB

#6 OBHOT

Box of Clues

Stumped? Maybe you can find a clue
below.

-Lincoln's small legal tender
-Coin collecting, for example
-Woodsy structure
-Writing sheet
-A, B, C, D...
-Toll-taker's structure
-Flying cloth

Arrange the circled letters
to solve the mystery answer.

MYSTERY ANSWER

MEANS THE SAME

JUMBLE. BrainBusters! Junior

Unscramble the Jumbles, one letter to each square, to spell pairs of words with the same or similar meanings.

For example:

HYSIN	BGRTIH
S H I N Y	B R I G H T

#1 HIHG — LTOYF

#2 AMRH — MAGEAD

#3 EUGH — NIESMEM

#4 UOLYS — EROTNT

#5 REUTP — EDOLEPX

Arrange the circled letters to solve the mystery answer.

MYSTERY ANSWER

CARNIVORES

JUMBLE BrainBusters! Junior

Unscramble the Jumbles, one letter to each square, to spell carnivores.

#1 LNIO

#2 ETIRG

#3 NHAEY

#4 CAAJLK

#5 ADBERG

#6 RLOEADP

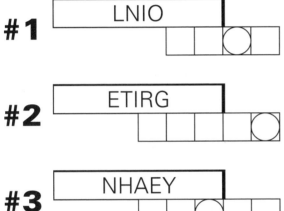

Carnivore

Carnivore is the term commonly applied to any animal whose diet consists wholly or largely of meat.

Over time, many carnivores have adapted to an omnivorous (mixed) diet.

Arrange the circled letters to solve the mystery answer.

MYSTERY ANSWER

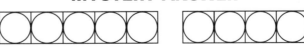

STARTS WITH A VOWEL

Unscramble the Jumbles, one letter to each square, to spell words that start with vowels (a,e,i,o,u).

#1 HEITG

#2 AETCX

#3 JNYEO

#4 EORRD

#5 MIPROT

#6 ASERWN

Arrange the circled letters to solve the mystery answer.

Box of Clues

Stumped? Maybe you can find a clue below.

-Arrangement, sequence
-The square root of 64
-Reply
-North or South _____
-Take pleasure in
-Precise
-Bring in from another country

MYSTERY ANSWER

SOUTH AMERICA

JUMBLE BrainBusters! Junior

Unscramble the Jumbles, one letter to each square, to spell words related to South America.

#1 CIELH

#2 VRIRE

#3 ZRILAB

#4 NAMOZA

#5 OILBIAV

#6 CEUORDA

Box of Clues

Stumped? Maybe you can find a clue below.

- Quito's home (starts with "E")
- _____ rain forest
- Home to Bogota (starts with "C")
- Largest South American country
- "Cold-sounding" country
- Home to La Paz (starts with "B")
- Amazon waterway

Arrange the circled letters to solve the mystery answer.

MYSTERY ANSWER

STARTS WITH "V"

Unscramble the Jumbles, one letter to each square, to spell words that start with "V".

#1 EVBR

#2 VIECO

#3 LIONIV

#4 AVINHS

#5 ANVILAL

#6 BIRVAET

Box of Clues

Stumped? Maybe you can find a clue below.

-Ice cream flavor
-Disappear
-Shake
-Stringed instrument
-Guest
-"Running," for example
-Human sound

Arrange the circled letters to solve the mystery answer.

MYSTERY ANSWER

FOOD

Unscramble the Jumbles, one letter to each square, to spell words related to food.

#1 EFBE

#2 OOIEKC

#3 TBRETU

Box of Clues

Stumped? Maybe you can find a clue below.

#4 FUMINF

-English _____
-Type of fruit
-Cow meat
-Mushy breakfast food
-Shaped ground beef
-Dairy additive
-Milk's common partner

#5 AABNNA

#6 AAOETLM

Arrange the circled letters to solve the mystery answer.

MYSTERY ANSWER

ALL ABOUT MONEY

Unscramble the Jumbles, one letter to each square, to spell words related to money.

#1 NAKB

#2 ODGL

#3 LVEUA

#4 CSOTK

#5 SIVNTE

#6 MAPNYTE

Box of Clues

Stumped? Maybe you can find a clue below.

- Commit money as to return a profit
- _____ account
- Financial institution
- Worth
- Valuable coin metal
- _____ certificate or common _____
- _____ plan; car _____

Arrange the circled letters to solve the mystery answer.

MYSTERY ANSWER

EUROPEAN COUNTRIES

Unscramble the Jumbles, one letter to each square, to spell names of European countries.

#1 NFCEAR

#2 APODLN

#3 TURAIAS

#4 MORNIAA

Box of Clues

Stumped? Maybe you can find a clue below.

-Home to Bucharest (starts with "R")
-Spain's northeastern neighbor (starts with "F")
-Home to Munich (starts with "G")
-Germany's eastern neighbor (starts with "P")
-Home to Lisbon (starts with "P")
-Home to Brussels (starts with "B")
-Alpine country (starts with "A")

#5 BMLUGIE

#6 MEGARYN

Arrange the circled letters to solve the mystery answer.

MYSTERY ANSWER

ALL ABOUT MUSIC

JUMBLE BrainBusters! Junior

Unscramble the Jumbles, one letter to each square, to spell words related to music.

#1 LUFET

#2 ALPOK

#3 MTEOP

Box of Clues

Stumped? Maybe you can find a clue below.

- Member of the oboe family
- Part of the musical staff between two bars
- Woodwind instrument
- Lively Bohemian dance music
- Rate of speed
- A musical scale, key, mode

#4 OAMRJ

#5 OSABONS

Arrange the circled letters to solve the mystery answer.

MYSTERY ANSWER

state
capitals

animals

JUMBLE

BrainBusters

Junior

ADVANCED
PUZZLES

human
body

outer
space

money

sports

BIRDS

Unscramble the Jumbles, one letter to each square, to spell types of birds.

#1 FCNIH

#2 NORIB

#3 OGEOS

#4 LALMDRA

Box of Clues

Stumped? Maybe you can find a clue below.

-Type of duck
-North American thrush
-Large waterfowl
-Large flightless bird
-Type of songbird
-Small parrot
-Pinkish-white bird

#5 AARETKEP

#6 MLAIFONG

Arrange the circled letters to solve the mystery answer.

MYSTERY ANSWER

SPORTS

Unscramble the Jumbles, one letter to each square, to spell words related to sports.

#1 CHPNU

#2 ORHME

#3 OIGALE

#4 REEJYS

#5 OLDEUB

#6 ACTECRH

Box of Clues

Stumped? Maybe you can find a clue below.

- Offensive boxing move
- A baseball position
- Arena
- Soccer or hockey position
- Uniform top
- A reason to trip
- Ground rule _____

Arrange the circled letters to solve the mystery answer.

MYSTERY ANSWER

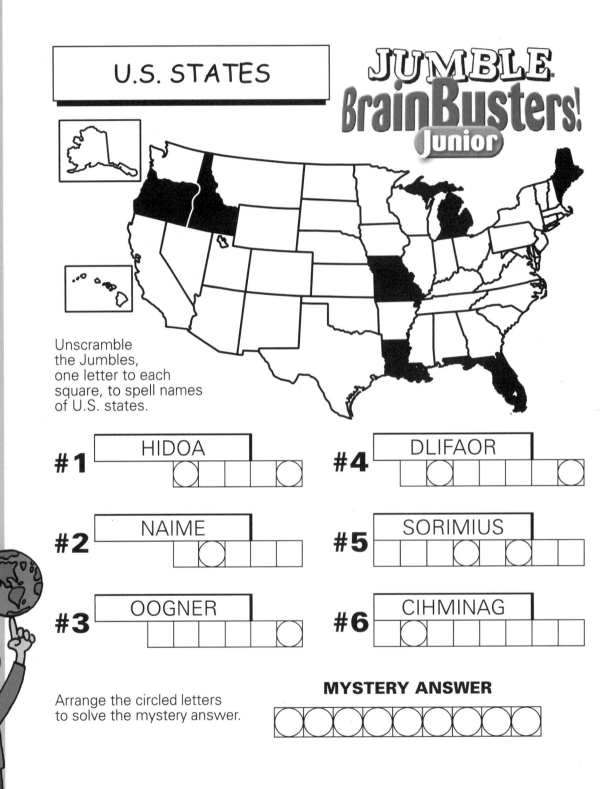

U.S. STATES

JUMBLE. BrainBusters! Junior

Unscramble the Jumbles, one letter to each square, to spell names of U.S. states.

#1 HIDOA

#2 NAIME

#3 OOGNER

#4 DLIFAOR

#5 SORIMIUS

#6 CIHMINAG

Arrange the circled letters to solve the mystery answer.

MYSTERY ANSWER

AUTOMOBILES

Unscramble the Jumbles, one letter to each square, to spell words related to automobiles.

#1 OHDO

#2 RCUTK

#3 EIWRP

Interesting Automobile Facts

#4 EWELH

Private cars were not allowed on Bermuda until 1948. Most people got around on bicycles.

#5 VDIRRE

More Americans have died in auto accidents than have died in all wars fought by the United States.

#6 CPIPKU

Arrange the circled letters to solve the mystery answer.

MYSTERY ANSWER

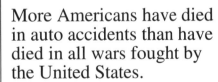

THE HUMAN BODY

Unscramble the Jumbles, one letter to each square, to spell words related to the human body.

#1 HIRA

#2 OEBN

#3 OTOF

#4 ANGDL

#5 TOHUM

#6 DKIYEN

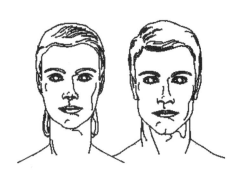

Interesting Human Body Facts

There are millions of digestive glands in the human stomach.

The human ear can distinguish from more than 1,000 musical tones.

Arrange the circled letters to solve the mystery answer.

MYSTERY ANSWER

BASEBALL

Unscramble the Jumbles, one letter to each square, to spell words related to baseball.

#1 AWKL

#2 TUUGOD

#3 BODLEU

#4 HPCREIT

#5 ADDIONM

#6 ANMARGE

Box of Clues

Stumped? Maybe you can find a clue below.

-Sitting area
-Leader, decision maker
-Reason to head to first
-Type of hit
-Warm-up area
-Field shape
-A position

Arrange the circled letters to solve the mystery answer.

MYSTERY ANSWER

MATH

JUMBLE BrainBusters! Junior

Unscramble the Jumbled letters, one letter to each square, so that each equation is correct.

For example: NONTEOEOW
ONE + ONE = TWO

#1 NFVIEEIEFOV

◯□□□ × ◯□□□□ = □□□□◯

#2 STXIVXSWELIE

□□◯ + ◯□□ = ◯□□□□□

#3 HTRETREEHEENO

□□□□□□ ÷ □□◯□ = ◯□□

#4 ROUFROFUIGTEH

□□◯□ + ◯□◯□ = □◯□□□

#5 HNNIERTELEWETEV

□□◯□ + □□◯□□ = □◯□□□□

Arrange the circled letters to solve the mystery equation.

MYSTERY EQUATION

◯◯◯◯◯ × ◯◯◯◯◯ = ◯◯◯◯◯◯◯◯

AROUND THE HOME

Unscramble the Jumbles, one letter to each square, to spell words related to things found around the home.

#1 VONE

#2 ATLEB

#3 HNOPE

#4 NPRYTA

Box of Clues

Stumped? Maybe you can find a clue below.

-Piece of furniture with a flat top
-Kitchen _____
-Communication device
-Type of opening
-Large closet near the kitchen
-Cooking chamber
-Light _____

#5 SCITWH

#6 NWIWOD

Arrange the circled letters to solve the mystery answer.

MYSTERY ANSWER

ADJECTIVES

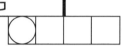
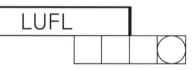

JUMBLE
BrainBusters!
Junior

Unscramble the Jumbles, one letter
to each square, to spell adjectives.

#1 HHIG

#2 LUFL

#3 WDIL

#4 TWIFS

#5 NLLYEO

#6 SGYOSL

"Bright"
"Sunny"
"Warm"

"Large"
"African"
"Asian"

"Strong"
"Muscular"
"Powerful"

An adjective is a word that modifies
a noun by describing it. An adjective
might indicate a noun's quantity or
extent, or specify a thing as distinct
from something else.

Box of Clues

Stumped? Maybe you can find a clue
below.

-Starts with "W"; ends with "D"

-Starts with "H"; ends with "H"

-Starts with "S"; ends with "T"

-Starts with "F"; ends with "L"

-Starts with "H"; ends with "W"

-Starts with "G"; ends with "Y"

-Starts with "L"; ends with "Y"

Arrange the circled letters
to solve the mystery answer.

MYSTERY ANSWER

U.S. CITIES

Unscramble the Jumbles, one letter to each square, to spell names of U.S. cities.

#1 AMIMI

#2 MOAAH

#3 AADLSL

#4 NABLYA

#5 ESTALET

#6 LOAADNK

Box of Clues

Stumped? Maybe you can find a clue below.

- San Francisco's neighbor across the bay
- Largest city and capital of Georgia
- South Florida city on the Atlantic
- Ft. Worth's neighbor
- Largest city in Washington state
- The capital of New York
- Largest city in Nebraska

Arrange the circled letters to solve the mystery answer.

MYSTERY ANSWER

AFRICAN COUNTRIES

Unscramble the Jumbles, one letter to each square, to spell names of African countries.

#1 BLIAY

#2 EKYAN

#3 AZIABM

#4 ARDAWN

#5 ELIABIR

#6 COORMOC

Box of Clues

Stumped? Maybe you can find a clue below.

-Starts with "Z"; ends with "A"
-Starts with "K"; ends with "A"
-Starts with "Z"; ends with "E"
-Starts with "R"; ends with "A"
-Starts with "L"; ends with "A"
-Starts with "M"; ends with "O"
-Starts with "L"; ends with "A"

Arrange the circled letters to solve the mystery answer.

MYSTERY ANSWER

ALL ABOUT MONEY

Unscramble the Jumbles, one letter to each square, to spell words related to money.

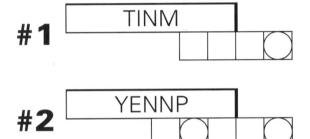

#1 TINM

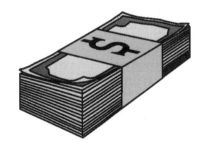

#2 YENNP

#3 OPUDN

#4 NISVTE

Box of Clues

Stumped? Maybe you can find a clue below.

-British currency
-Type of coin
-Commit money as to return a profit
-Government department in charge of finances
-Pay later
-U.S. currency
-Create a coin out of metal

#5 LODRAL

#6 HCRAEG

Arrange the circled letters to solve the mystery answer.

MYSTERY ANSWER

ALL ABOUT PLANTS

Unscramble the Jumbles, one letter to each square, to spell words related to plants.

#1 ERTE

#2 ENFR

#3 GLTIH

Box of Clues

Stumped? Maybe you can find a clue below.

- The study of plants
- Mass of leaves on a plant
- Woody plant that lives for many years
- Large class of flowerless plants
- Pine _____
- Desert plant
- Bright photosynthesis component

#4 EELNED

#5 TOBAYN

#6 CCASUT

Arrange the circled letters to solve the mystery answer.

MYSTERY ANSWER

FOOD

JUMBLE.
BrainBusters!
Junior

Unscramble the Jumbles, one letter
to each square, to spell words related
to food.

#1 RIUTF

#2 LERSIH

#3 RUEBRG

#4 REPEPP

Interesting Food Facts

The number of burgers sold
by McDonald's is more than
10 times the number of
people on Earth.

General Mills introduced
Trix cereal in 1954.

#5 TPEELZR

#6 ESAODOF

Arrange the circled letters
to solve the mystery answer.

MYSTERY ANSWER

PLANET EARTH

Unscramble the Jumbles, one letter to each square, to spell words related to planet Earth.

#1 RRIEV

#2 ALUFT

#3 EBCHA

#4 AMWPS

#5 ASENOS

#6 TOMNINAU

Arrange the circled letters to solve the mystery answer.

Box of Clues

Stumped? Maybe you can find a clue below.

-Winter or spring
-Break in the Earth's crust
-Mass of air
-High, projecting landmass
-Grand Canyon creator
-Shoreline
-Wet area

MYSTERY ANSWER

MUSICAL INSTRUMENTS

Unscramble the Jumbles, one letter to each square, to spell names of musical instruments.

#1 OEOB

#2 RDMU

#3 LUETF

#4 NIOILV

#5 NEORTC

#6 SAOBNOS

Box of Clues

Stumped? Maybe you can find a clue below.

-Percussion instrument
-Small trumpet
-Woodwind instrument
-Brass instrument with a movable slide
-Woodwind instrument
-Stringed instrument
-Woodwind instrument

Arrange the circled letters to solve the mystery answer.

MYSTERY ANSWER

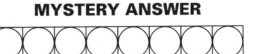

SOUTH AMERICA

JUMBLE BrainBusters! Junior

Unscramble the Jumbles, one letter to each square, to spell words related to South America.

#1 RZIBLA

#2 VBIOLIA

#3 CIPAICF

#4 GURAUYU

#5 RCAAASC

#6 NALATICT

Arrange the circled letters to solve the mystery answer.

Box of Clues

Stumped? Maybe you can find a clue below.

-Home to Rio de Janeiro
-Home to Montevideo (starts with "U")
-Venezuela's capital (starts with "C", ends with "S")
-Western border
-Home to La Paz (starts with "B")
-Eastern border
-The capital of Chile (starts with "S", ends with "O")

MYSTERY ANSWER

AMERICAN INDIANS

Unscramble the Jumbles, one letter to each square, to spell names of American Indian tribes.

#1 AAPCEH

#2 VNAOAJ

#3 PLUEOB

#4 WMHOKA

#5 OHIMANC

#6 NHSAEEW

Arrange the circled letters to solve the mystery answer.

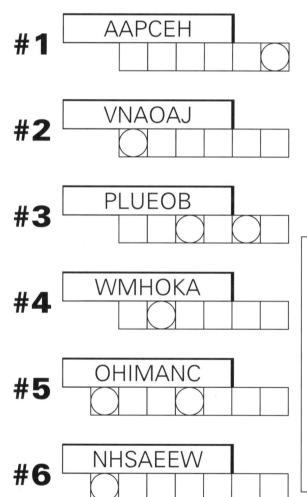

Box of Clues

Stumped? Maybe you can find a clue below.

-Starts with "P"; ends with "O"
-Starts with "M"; ends with "K"
-Starts with "S"; ends with "E"
-Starts with "S"; ends with "E"
-Starts with "N"; ends with "O"
-Starts with "A"; ends with "E"
-Starts with "M"; ends with "N"

MYSTERY ANSWER

U.S. STATES

Unscramble the Jumbles, one letter to each square, to spell names of U.S. states.

#1 AIOW

#2 DHOIA

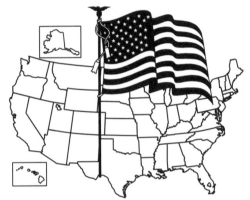

#3 NSKAAS

#4 ROONGE

Interesting U.S. State Facts

New Jersey was named for the English Channel island of Jersey.

The name Kansas comes from the Sioux Indian word that most likely meant "people of the south wind."

#5 AAAAMBL

Arrange the circled letters to solve the mystery answer.

MYSTERY ANSWER

CLOTHING

Unscramble the Jumbles, one letter to each square, to spell words related to clothing.

#1 RSDES

#2 OGVEL

#3 AFBICR

#4 UTBNOT

#5 MUFIONR

#6 TSEERAW

Box of Clues

Stumped? Maybe you can find a clue below.

-Hand covering
-Fastener
-Material
-Team member garment
-An article of clothing
-Cool weather garment
-Gown

Arrange the circled letters to solve the mystery answer.

MYSTERY ANSWER

SPORTS TEAMS

Unscramble the Jumbles, one letter to each square, to spell names of professional sports teams.

#1 GRITSE

#2 YFRSEL

#3 GAEESL

#4 DARIRES

#5 PTINSOS

#6 RAIWZDS

Box of Clues

Stumped? Maybe you can find a clue below.

- Pennsylvania football team
- California baseball team
- Detroit baseball team
- Pennsylvania hockey team
- California football team
- Detroit basketball team
- Washington, D.C., basketball team

Arrange the circled letters to solve the mystery answer.

MYSTERY ANSWER

PLANET EARTH

Unscramble the Jumbles, one letter to each square, to spell words related to planet Earth.

#1 VECA

#2 RRIEV

#3 BOLGE

#4 ALEVYL

#5 NJEUGL

#6 ALGONO

Box of Clues

Stumped? Maybe you can find a clue below.

- Earth's round shape
- Shallow body of water
- Large stream of water
- Explosive vent
- Warm forest
- Low area
- Underground chamber

Arrange the circled letters to solve the mystery answer.

MYSTERY ANSWER

COUNTRIES

JUMBLE
BrainBusters!
Junior

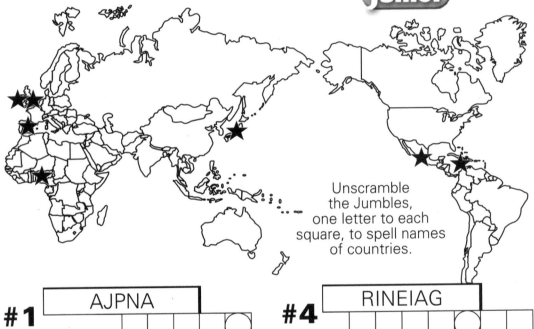

Unscramble
the Jumbles,
one letter to each
square, to spell names
of countries.

#1 AJPNA

#4 RINEIAG

#2 ARCENF

#5 AAMIJCA

#3 EMIOCX

#6 NEGNADL

Arrange the circled letters
to solve the mystery answer.

MYSTERY ANSWER

MAMMALS

Unscramble the Jumbles, one letter to each square, to spell names of mammals.

#1 YHNAE

#2 HIPCM

#3 ALMAL

#4 OMEOS

Box of Clues

Stumped? Maybe you can find a clue below.

-Starts with "M"; ends with "E"
-Starts with "C"; ends with "P"
-Starts with "P"; ends with "R"
-Starts with "C"; ends with "E"
-Starts with "G"; ends with "E"
-Starts with "H"; ends with "A"
-Starts with "L"; ends with "A"

#5 OYOTEC

#6 FRGAIEF

Arrange the circled letters to solve the mystery answer.

MYSTERY ANSWER

U.S. PRESIDENTS

Unscramble the Jumbles, one letter to each square, to spell last names of U.S. presidents.

#1 FTTA

#2 OKPL

#3 DAASM

#4 AREGNA

#5 CLINNLO

#6 HOSOJNN

Box of Clues

Stumped? Maybe you can find a clue below.

-40th U.S. president
-James Knox _____
-This president was assassinated while in office
-Seventh U.S. president
-John _____
-The "J" in "L.B.J."
-William Howard _____

Arrange the circled letters to solve the mystery answer.

MYSTERY ANSWER

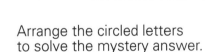

MATH

JUMBLE BrainBusters! Junior

Unscramble the Jumbled
letters, one letter to each square,
so that each equation is correct.

For example:
NONTEOEOW
O N E + O N E = T W O

#1 FRNOUUOEORF

☐☐☐☐☐ × ☐☐◯ = ☐☐☐☐◯

#2 WTOETENTNYTW

☐◯ × ☐◯ = ☐☐◯☐☐

#3 HIGETOGNIETHE

◯☐☐☐☐ ÷ ◯☐☐ = ☐☐☐☐◯

#4 NNEOENOEOOERZ

☐☐☐☐ × ☐◯☐ = ☐☐◯☐ + ☐◯☐

#5 NIXEERTERZEOZOS

☐☐☐◯☐☐☐ × ◯☐☐☐ = ◯☐☐☐

Arrange the circled letters
to solve the mystery equation.

MYSTERY EQUATION

◯◯◯◯ × ◯◯◯ = ◯◯◯ × ◯◯◯◯

149

COUNTRIES

JUMBLE
BrainBusters!
Junior

Unscramble
the Jumbles,
one letter to each
square, to spell names
of countries.

#1 HCIEL

#2 CAAADN

#3 CEMIOX

#4 AAMNPA

#5 AONYWR

#6 OBILIAV

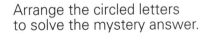

Arrange the circled letters
to solve the mystery answer.

MYSTERY ANSWER

ADVERBS

JUMBLE.
BrainBusters!
Junior

"The runner ran quickly."
"The runner ran slowly."

An adverb is a word used to modify
a verb, an adjective, another adverb,
a preposition, a phrase, a clause or
a sentence. It is often used to show
degree, manner, place, or time.

Unscramble the Jumbles, one letter
to each square, to spell adverbs.

#1 MDIYL

#2 CNLIYE

#3 FOSLYT

#4 RFILYM

#5 POELYN

#6 LRCUEDY

Box of Clues

Stumped? Maybe you can find a clue
below.

-Tightly, solidly
-In an unrefined manner
-In an obscure manner; with
 little light
-In an exposed manner
-Well, properly; in a friendly
 manner
-In a high-handed, pompous
 manner
-Gently, lightly

Arrange the circled letters
to solve the mystery answer.

MYSTERY ANSWER

DOGS

Unscramble the Jumbles, one letter to each square, to spell words related to dogs.

#1 UHYSK

#2 OBEXR

#3 AELBEG

#4 PIANLES

#5 DLBUOLG

#6 PSEHEDHR

Box of Clues

Stumped? Maybe you can find a clue below.

-Starts with "S"; ends with "D"

-Starts with "G"; ends with "D"

-Starts with "S"; ends with "L"

-Starts with "H"; ends with "Y"

-Starts with "B"; ends with "G"

-Starts with "B"; ends with "E"

-Starts with "B"; ends with "R"

Arrange the circled letters to solve the mystery answer.

MYSTERY ANSWER

FAMOUS ATHLETES

Unscramble the Jumbles, one letter to each square, to spell last names of famous athletes.

#1 DIBR

#2 GIKN

#3 OBGR

#4 NBCEH

Box of Clues

Stumped? Maybe you can find a clue below.

-Johnny _____
-Lou _____
-Ben _____
-Larry _____
-Bjorn _____
-Betsy or Billie Jean _____
-Yogi _____

#5 ERARB

#6 OHANG

Arrange the circled letters to solve the mystery answer.

MYSTERY ANSWER

TIME LINE

Unscramble the Jumbles, one letter to each square, to spell words as suggested by the time line.

#1 **1914** _____ Canal opens

#2 **1961** South _____ becomes a republic

#3 **1962** Missile _____ in Cuba

#4 **1972** _____ calculator invented

#5 **1979** Thatcher becomes _____ prime minister

#6 **1990** Lech Walesa becomes president of _____

#1 AANPMA

#2 FAIACR

#3 CISISR

#4 OCEPTK

#5 TRIBIHS

#6 LPNODA

Arrange the circled letters to solve the mystery answer.

1982 _____ invented

MYSTERY ANSWER

ASIAN COUNTRIES

JUMBLE BrainBusters! Junior

Unscramble the Jumbles, one letter to each square, to spell names of Asian countries.

#1 NIAID

#2 SIARY

#3 SRIUAS

#4 NVTMEIA

#5 SPAINKAT

#6 LONMAIOG

Box of Clues

Stumped? Maybe you can find a clue below.

-Large, northern country
-Home to Hanoi
-India's western neighbor
-Turkey's southern neighbor
-Island south of Malaysia
-Russia's southern neighbor, China's northern neighbor
-Home to Calcutta

Arrange the circled letters to solve the mystery answer.

MYSTERY ANSWER

U.S. PRESIDENTS

Unscramble the Jumbles, one letter to each square, to spell last names of U.S. presidents.

#1 TFTA

#2 ODRF

#3 TRHARU

#4 GREANA

#5 EOHOVR

#6 NJSONOH

Box of Clues

Stumped? Maybe you can find a clue below.

-Starts with "F"; ends with "D"
-Starts with "A"; ends with "R"
-Starts with "J"; ends with "N"
-Starts with "H"; ends with "R"
-Starts with "T"; ends with "T"
-Starts with "J"; ends with "N"
-Starts with "R"; ends with "N"

Arrange the circled letters to solve the mystery answer.

MYSTERY ANSWER

POETRY

Unscramble the Jumbles, one letter to each square, to spell words found in the poem.

#1 YOSLLW

#2 CNIETO

#3 ZRAIEEL

#4 ARDBN

#5 CSODNE

TIME by Kim Nolan

Minutes tick so _____ #1
Yet hours slip away
Before you even _____ #2
It's a whole new day

Weeks drag on forever
Yet months just disappear
Then you stop and _____ #3
It's a _____ #4 new year

Time is very clever
First slow then fast
It only takes a _____ #5
Then present becomes past

Arrange the circled letters to solve the mystery answer. (The mystery answer is not in the poem.)

MYSTERY ANSWER

FAMOUS PEOPLE

Unscramble the Jumbles, one letter
to each square, to spell last names of
famous people.

#1 AOSS

#2 WTINA

#3 ODWOS

#4 ROAJND

Box of Clues

Stumped? Maybe you can find a clue
below.

-Singer Whitney
-Golfing Tiger
-Michael _____
-Sammy _____
-Author Mark (1835-1910)
-Popular singer, actress
-Ricky _____

#5 RAMINT

#6 OHSUONT

Arrange the circled letters
to solve the mystery answer.

MYSTERY ANSWER

ELEMENTS

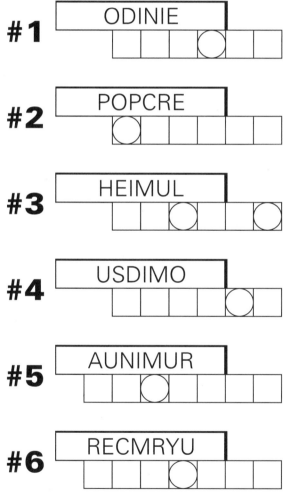

Unscramble the Jumbles, one letter to each square, to spell names of elements.

#1 ODINIE

#2 POPCRE

#3 HEIMUL

#4 USDIMO

#5 AUNIMUR

#6 RECMRYU

Arrange the circled letters to solve the mystery answer.

JUMBLE BrainBusters! Junior

An element is a fundamental substance consisting of atoms of only one kind that cannot be broken down into simpler substances.

THE PERIODIC TABLE

Box of Clues

Stumped? Maybe you can find a clue below.

-Starts with "U"; ends with "M"
-Starts with "S"; ends with "M"
-Starts with "I"; ends with "E"
-Starts with "M"; ends with "Y"
-Starts with "C"; ends with "M"
-Starts with "C"; ends with "R"
-Starts with "H"; ends with "M"

MYSTERY ANSWER

OUTER SPACE

Unscramble the Jumbles, one letter to each square, to spell words related to outer space.

#1 NLURA

#2 RAUSNU

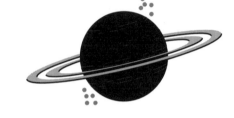

#3 TSYMES

Box of Clues

Stumped? Maybe you can find a clue below.

-Solar or lunar _____
-Saturn's outer neighbor
-Of or relating to the moon
-Attractive force
-Solar _____
-Cosmos
-_____ Borealis

#4 UARARO

#5 CELIEPS

#6 VGAIRYT

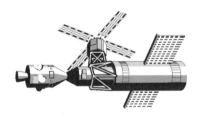

Arrange the circled letters to solve the mystery answer.

MYSTERY ANSWER

ABBREVIATIONS

Unscramble the Jumbles, one letter to each square, to spell words that are often abbreviated.

#1 NJIROU

An abbreviation is a shortened form of a written word or phrase used in place of the whole.

#2 VAEUNE

#3 GASTUU

#4 WRPAAYK

#5 TSUDYAAR

#6 BVOENERM

Arrange the circled letters to solve the mystery answer.

MYSTERY ANSWER

THE HUMAN BODY

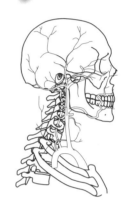

Unscramble the Jumbles, one letter to each square, to spell words related to the human body.

#1 AINRB

#2 HCETS

#3 LODBO

#4 KEYNID

#5 PESNEL

#6 OUETGN

Arrange the circled letters to solve the mystery answer.

Box of Clues

Stumped? Maybe you can find a clue below.

-Starts with "C"; ends with "T"
-Starts with "K"; ends with "Y"
-Starts with "B"; ends with "E"
-Starts with "B"; ends with "D"
-Starts with "T"; ends with "E"
-Starts with "B"; ends with "N"
-Starts with "S"; ends with "N"

MYSTERY ANSWER

MEANS THE OPPOSITE

JUMBLE
BrainBusters!
Junior

Unscramble the Jumbles, one letter to each square, to spell pairs of words with opposite meanings.

For example:

EIDW		NOAWRR
W I D E		N A R R O W

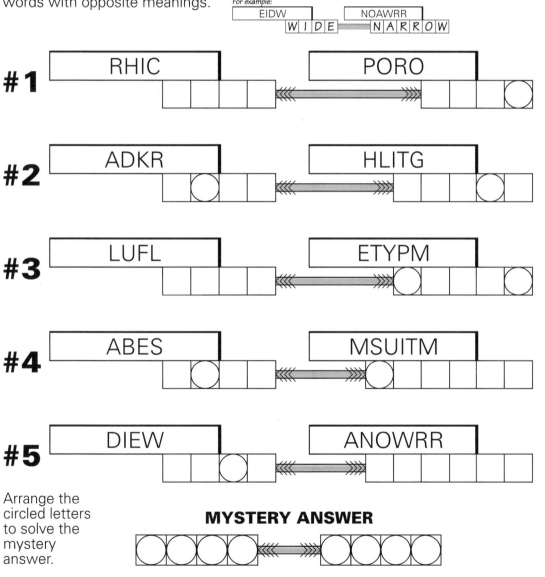

#1 RHIC ⫷⫸ PORO

#2 ADKR ⫷⫸ HLITG

#3 LUFL ⫷⫸ ETYPM

#4 ABES ⫷⫸ MSUITM

#5 DIEW ⫷⫸ ANOWRR

Arrange the circled letters to solve the mystery answer.

MYSTERY ANSWER

○○○○ ⫷⫸ ○○○○

STARTS WITH "W"

Unscramble the Jumbles, one letter to each square, to spell words that start with "W".

#1 EWGED

#2 RNECWH

#3 SWIULHF

#4 DWIENDG

#5 EKEWAYD

#6 EMLCOEW

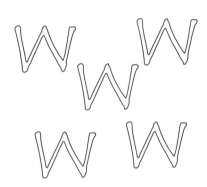

Box of Clues

Stumped? Maybe you can find a clue below.

-Type of ceremony
-Tapered piece
-Monday
-Gripping tool
-_____ mat
-Hurt
-Hopeful

Arrange the circled letters to solve the mystery answer.

MYSTERY ANSWER

164

LARGE CITIES

JUMBLE BrainBusters! Junior

Unscramble the Jumbles, one letter to each square, to spell names of large cities.

#1
DSEYNY

#2
NOLDNO

#3
MBOBYA

#4
AWASWR

#5
CAHIOCG

#6
THOSUNO

Box of Clues

Stumped? Maybe you can find a clue below.

-Starts with "H"; ends with "N"
-Starts with "L"; ends with "N"
-Starts with "S"; ends with "Y"
-Starts with "B"; ends with "Y"
-Starts with "W"; ends with "W"
-Starts with "B"; ends with "D"
-Starts with "C"; ends with "O"

Arrange the circled letters to solve the mystery answer.

MYSTERY ANSWER

CLOTHING

Unscramble the Jumbles, one letter to each square, to spell words related to clothing.

#1 PAAKR

#2 ESDSR

#3 EJNSA

#4 CJEATK

#5 ASDNAL

#6 MTINET

Arrange the circled letters to solve the mystery answer.

Interesting Clothing Facts

Almost 50 percent of Americans own at least one piece of clothing with a professional sports team's logo on it.

Harry Truman worked at a clothing store before becoming president of the United States.

MYSTERY ANSWER

STARTS WITH A VOWEL

Unscramble the Jumbles, one letter to each square, to spell words that start with vowels (a,e,i,o,u).

#1 AIAS

#2 DIAOH

#3 NUINO

#4 DUTAL

#5 FNUIRA

#6 GOAERN

Box of Clues

Stumped? Maybe you can find a clue below.

- Association, league
- Large landmass
- Type of fruit
- Unjust
- A U.S. state
- Home to about 50 million
- Fully-grown person

Arrange the circled letters to solve the mystery answer.

MYSTERY ANSWER

THE HUMAN BODY

Unscramble the Jumbles, one letter to each square, to spell words related to the human body.

#1 LGADN

#2 EPISVL

#3 OTRXAH

#4 ETONND

#5 USMECL

#6 ARCETAH

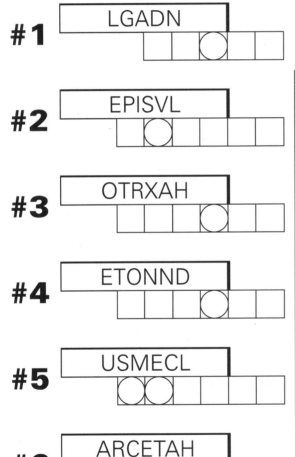

Box of Clues

Stumped? Maybe you can find a clue below.

- Strength-producing tissue
- Adrenal _____
- Basin-shaped structure in the skeleton
- Tough band of connective tissue
- Chest area
- Thin membrane that carries sound
- Windpipe

Arrange the circled letters to solve the mystery answer.

MYSTERY ANSWER

NOUNS

Unscramble the Jumbles, one letter to each square, to spell nouns.

#1 OBKO

#2 CURTK

#3 RWODL

#4 AONWG

#5 ECTKIT

#6 COFIEF

Arrange the circled letters to solve the mystery answer.

"Animal"
"Dinosaur"
"Reptile"

"Runner"
"Athlete"
"Racer"

"Tree"
"Plant"
"Cypress"

A noun is *a word that is the name of something (as in a person, animal, place, thing, quality, idea or action).*

Box of Clues

Stumped? Maybe you can find a clue below.

-_____ stop
-Telephone _____
-Apartment _____
-Speeding _____
-Patent _____; Oval _____
-_____ train
-_____ Series

MYSTERY ANSWER

ANIMALS

JUMBLE
BrainBusters!
Junior

Unscramble the Jumbles, one letter to each square, to spell names of animals.

#1 ACBR

#2 OEML

#3 OKSTR

#4 YOCEOT

#5 ROIGLAL

#6 TANEPRH

Interesting Animal Facts

There is a type of bat called a microbat. This type of bat weighs less than one ounce.

There is a type of earthworm in Australia that can grow to more than 10 feet in length.

Arrange the circled letters to solve the mystery answer.

MYSTERY ANSWER

U.S. CITIES

JUMBLE BrainBusters! Junior

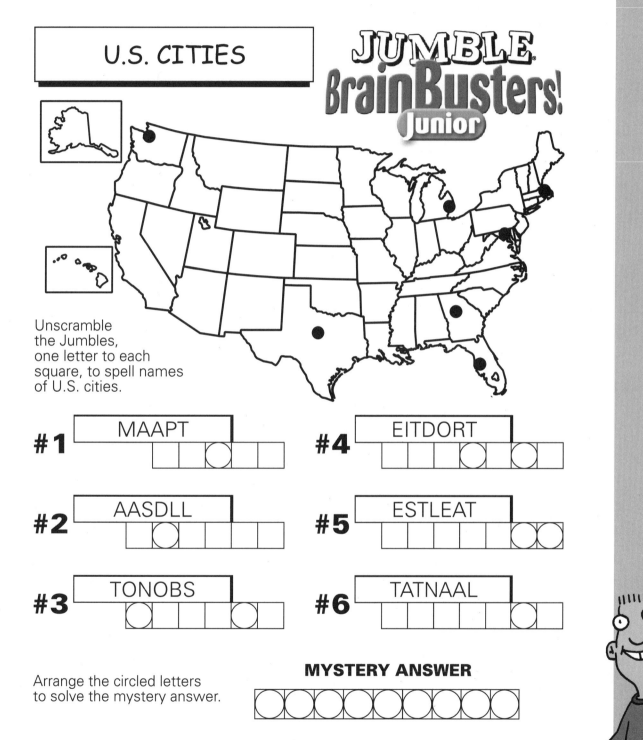

Unscramble the Jumbles, one letter to each square, to spell names of U.S. cities.

#1 MAAPT

#2 AASDLL

#3 TONOBS

#4 EITDORT

#5 ESTLEAT

#6 TATNAAL

Arrange the circled letters to solve the mystery answer.

MYSTERY ANSWER

ADJECTIVES

Unscramble the Jumbles, one letter to each square, to spell adjectives.

#1 EELVL

#2 RSYTU

#3 TESPE

#4 UGYNO

#5 LTLEIT

#6 DARNMO

"Bright"
"Sunny"
"Warm"

"Large"
"African"
"Asian"

"Strong"
"Muscular"
"Powerful"

An adjective is a word that modifies a noun by describing it. An adjective might indicate a noun's quantity or extent, or specify a thing as distinct from something else.

Arrange the circled letters to solve the mystery answer.

MYSTERY ANSWER

Box of Clues

Stumped? Maybe you can find a clue below.

-Starts with "Y"; ends with "G"

-Starts with "L"; ends with "E"

-Starts with "R"; ends with "Y"

-Starts with "S"; ends with "P"

-Starts with "G"; ends with "E"

-Starts with "R"; ends with "M"

-Starts with "L"; ends with "L"

GEORGE WASHINGTON

Unscramble the Jumbles, one letter to each square, to spell words related to George Washington.

#1 HEFRNC

#2 RATMAH

#3 TVIRCOY

#4 NUCORYT

#5 GIRIVIAN

#6 REELDAAW

Box of Clues

Stumped? Maybe you can find a clue below.

-Washington's enemy in 1754
-Washington's birth state
-Mrs. Washington
-River crossed in 1776
-Washington estate
-Washington's end result
 battling Cornwallis
-"The Father of His _____"

Arrange the circled letters to solve the mystery answer.

MYSTERY ANSWER

SPORTS

Unscramble the Jumbles, one letter to each square, to spell words related to sports.

#1 CEURV

#2 SIKIGN

#3 ENISTN

#4 HTOYPR

#5 RFAAIYW

#6 AMAERNG

Arrange the circled letters to solve the mystery answer.

Box of Clues

Stumped? Maybe you can find a clue below.

- Golfer's goal off the tee
- Winner's prize
- Downhill sport
- Type of pitch
- Sport's outfit
- Head baseball coach
- A racket sport

MYSTERY ANSWER

WEATHER

Unscramble the Jumbles, one letter to each square, to spell words related to weather.

#1 HILA

#2 DILM

#3 LCIHYL

#4 NCLYEOC

#5 GDOHTUR

#6 ZBIZRDAL

Box of Clues

Stumped? Maybe you can find a clue below.

-Windy winter storm
-Circular storm
-Falling lumps of ice
-Comfortably warm
-Weather conditions over an extended period of time
-Uncomfortably cool
-Extended dry spell

Arrange the circled letters to solve the mystery answer.

MYSTERY ANSWER

POETRY

Unscramble the Jumbles, one letter to each square, to spell words found in the poem.

#1 NIMD

#2 ANLSW

#3 HIWEL

#4 RWOG

#5 RSIPGN

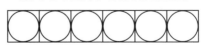

SPRING by Kim Nolan

Weather transforms
Changing its _____ #1
Yesterday it was cruel
Today it is kind

Flowers bloom
And _____ #2 turn green
Children play outside
_____ #3 parents clean

Trees _____ #4 leaves
And robins sing
Goodbye winter
Hello _____ #5

Arrange the circled letters to solve the mystery answer. (The mystery answer is not in the poem.)

MYSTERY ANSWER

ELEMENTS

Unscramble the Jumbles, one letter to each square, to spell names of elements.

#1 ZCIN

#2 LOGD

#3 LUFSRU

#4 GOYNXE

#5 OCBLTA

#6 SLCINIO

Arrange the circled letters to solve the mystery answer.

An element is a fundamental substance consisting of atoms of only one kind that cannot be broken down into simpler substances.

THE PERIODIC TABLE

Box of Clues

Stumped? Maybe you can find a clue below.

-Starts with "S"; ends with "N"
-Starts with "G"; ends with "D"
-Starts with "S"; ends with "R"
-Starts with "Z"; ends with "C"
-Starts with "N"; ends with "N"
-Starts with "C"; ends with "T"
-Starts with "O"; ends with "N"

MYSTERY ANSWER

MAMMALS

Unscramble the Jumbles, one letter to each square, to spell names of mammals.

#1 APDAN

#2 GAAJRU

#3 RFEETR

#4 LGROIAL

#5 MRSATKU

#6 HEPENTAL

Interesting Mammal Facts

Rodents make up the largest order of mammals. There are about 1,700 species of rodents.

The blue whale is the world's largest mammal.

Arrange the circled letters to solve the mystery answer.

MYSTERY ANSWER

COUNTRIES

Unscramble the Jumbles, one letter to each square, to spell names of countries.

#1 AINID

#2 AAAPNM

#3 RINIAEG

#4 RASIATU

#5 LIEADCN

#6 AEDKRMN

Box of Clues

Stumped? Maybe you can find a clue below.

- Home to an important canal
- Cold-sounding island country
- African country on the Atlantic coast
- Populous country in southern Asia
- India's western neighbor
- Home to Copenhagen
- Home to Vienna and Innsbruck

Arrange the circled letters to solve the mystery answer.

MYSTERY ANSWER

ANIMALS

JUMBLE BrainBusters! Junior

Unscramble the Jumbles, one letter to each square, to spell names of animals.

#1 UKSNK

#2 ACEML

#3 BRITBA

#4 TERLTU

#5 ROHGEP

#6 EOYKMN

Box of Clues

Stumped? Maybe you can find a clue below.

-Desert mammal
-Weasel relative
-Squirrel relative with stripes
-Primate mammal
-Burrowing rodent
-Toothless reptile
-Burrowing mammal with long ears

Arrange the circled letters to solve the mystery answer.

MYSTERY ANSWER

MATH

JUMBLE BrainBusters! Junior

Unscramble the Jumbled
letters, one letter to each square,
so that each equation is correct.

For example: NONTEOEOW
ONE + ONE = TWO

#1 WTFORUOWTO
○ ○ ÷ □ ○ = □□□

#2 RSTIWOXTEHE
□○ ÷ □○ = □○□

#3 NEOSEVESEENNV
□○ × □○ = □○□

#4 HRREETIEETNNHE
□□○ × □□□ = □○□

#5 RWVFETOEINTEOZ
○□□ × □□ = □○ + □□○

Arrange the circled letters
to solve the mystery equation.

MYSTERY EQUATION

○○○ × ○○○ = ○○○○ − ○○○○

U.S. STATE CAPITALS

Unscramble the Jumbles, one letter to each square, to spell U.S. state capitals.

#1 OIBES

#2 AALNYB

#3 OHEIXPN

#4 AALTNAT

#5 CJAONKS

#6 NCOODRC

Box of Clues

Stumped? Maybe you can find a clue below.

- The capital of Mississippi
- The capital of New Hampshire
- The capital of Idaho
- The capital of Georgia
- The capital of New York
- The capital of Nebraska
- The capital of Arizona

Arrange the circled letters to solve the mystery answer.

MYSTERY ANSWER

ANSWERS

1. **Jumbles: #1.** HELENA **#2.** JUNEAU **#3.** ATLANTA **#4.** TRENTON **#5.** OLYMPIA
   Answer: HONOLULU

2. **Jumbles: #1.** HAIR **#2.** HEAD **#3.** BONE **#4.** FOOT **#5.** TOOTH **#6.** THUMB
   Answer: THROAT

3. **Jumbles: #1.** CITY **#2.** HORN **#3.** CLOCK **#4.** TOOTH **#5.** MUSIC **#6.** MONTH
   Answer: SCHOOL

4. **Jumbles: #1.** IRON **#2.** BORON **#3.** COBALT **#4.** SODIUM **#5.** CALCIUM
   Answer: URANIUM

5. **Jumbles: #1.** TWO + TWO = FOUR
   #2. FIVE + FIVE = TEN
   #3. EIGHT + ONE = NINE
   #4. FOUR − THREE = ONE
   #5. THREE + ZERO = THREE
   Answer: ONE + THREE = FOUR

6. **Jumbles: #1.** HIPPO **#2.** MOOSE **#3.** TURKEY **#4.** WALRUS **#5.** GIRAFFE **#6.** CHICKEN
   Answer: ELEPHANT

7. **Jumbles: #1.** CROWN **#2.** CROWD **#3.** CACTUS **#4.** COFFEE **#5.** CLIMAX **#6.** CAPITAL
   Answer: CENTRAL

8. **Jumbles: #1.** HARP **#2.** FLUTE **#3.** BANJO **#4.** GUITAR **#5.** PICCOLO **#6.** TRUMPET
   Answer: CLARINET

9. **Jumbles: #1.** PIZZA **#2.** TOAST **#3.** SUGAR **#4.** CANDY **#5.** DONUT **#6.** PICKLE
   Answer: POPCORN

10. **Jumbles: #1.** OHIO **#2.** IDAHO **#3.** MAINE **#4.** NEVADA **#5.** KANSAS
    Answer: INDIANA

11. **Jumbles: #1.** FOUL **#2.** CATCH **#3.** COACH **#4.** BOXING **#5.** TACKLE **#6.** BASKET
    Answer: BASEBALL

12. **Jumbles: #1.** WARM **#2.** FRONT **#3.** SUNNY **#4.** FOGGY **#5.** CHILLY **#6.** FREEZE
    Answer: FORECAST

13. **Jumbles: #1.** TAFT **#2.** HAYES **#3.** GRANT **#4.** TAYLOR **#5.** HARDING **#6.** HARRISON
    Answer: GARFIELD

14. **Jumbles: #1.** CHILE **#2.** RUSSIA **#3.** BRAZIL **#4.** TURKEY **#5.** CANADA **#6.** MEXICO
    Answer: AUSTRALIA

15. **Jumbles: #1.** ITALY **#2.** IGLOO **#3.** ALLEY **#4.** OLDER **#5.** AWAKE **#6.** AFRAID
    Answer: ILLEGAL

16. **Jumbles: #1.** HILL **#2.** LAND **#3.** RIVER **#4.** CRUST **#5.** VALLEY **#6.** LAGOON
    Answer: ISLAND

17. **Jumbles: #1.** FIGHT **#2.** FLOCK **#3.** FLOOR **#4.** FROZEN **#5.** FALCON **#6.** FREEDOM
    Answer: FINLAND

18. **Jumbles: #1.** CAIRO **#2.** BERLIN **#3.** LONDON **#4.** MADRID **#5.** DETROIT **#6.** ATLANTA
    Answer: TORONTO

19. **Jumbles: #1.** CUBA **#2.** LIBYA **#3.** RUSSIA **#4.** POLAND **#5.** VIETNAM **#6.** GERMANY
    Answer: PORTUGAL

20. **Jumbles: #1.** HOME HOUSE **#2.** SOFT GENTLE **#3.** PRIZE AWARD **#4.** RAPID SPEEDY **#5.** LAUGH CACKLE
    Answer: DAMP SOGGY

21. **Jumbles: #1.** FOUL **#2.** GUARD **#3.** JERSEY **#4.** BASKET **#5.** PENALTY **#6.** OFFENSE
    Answer: REFEREE

22. **Jumbles: #1.** BLACK TRACK **#2.** LUNCH BUNCH **#3.** KNOCK STOCK **#4.** HABIT RABBIT **#5.** HEDGE PLEDGE
    Answer: RICK PICK

23. **Jumbles: #1.** ORBIT **#2.** PLUTO **#3.** COMET **#4.** SATURN **#5.** URANUS **#6.** JUPITER
    Answer: NEPTUNE

24. **Jumbles: #1.** GUITAR **#2.** GREECE **#3.** GROUND **#4.** GAMBLE **#5.** GRUMPY **#6.** GROWTH
    Answer: GARBAGE

25. **Jumbles: #1.** FLIGHT **#2.** VIETNAM **#3.** KENNEDY **#4.** POLAND **#5.** KUWAIT **#6.** RUSSIA
    Answer: GERMANY

26. **Jumbles: #1.** CHILDREN **#2.** UPTOWN **#3.** PEOPLE **#4.** HOME **#5.** WINTER
    Answer: WINTERTIME

27. **Jumbles: #1.** HAND **#2.** ANKLE **#3.** CHEST **#4.** MOUTH **#5.** KIDNEY **#6.** STOMACH
    Answer: SKELETON

28. **Jumbles: #1.** RICH **#2.** TINY **#3.** NICE **#4.** TALL **#5.** SOFT **#6.** BOLD
    Answer: ROTTEN

29. **Jumbles: #1.** CASH **#2.** VAULT **#3.** CHECK **#4.** PENNY **#5.** DOLLAR **#6.** CHARGE
    Answer: CURRENCY

30. **Jumbles: #1.** SEED **#2.** FERN **#3.** TRUNK **#4.** BLOOM **#5.** WOODS **#6.** NEEDLE
    Answer: FLOWER

31. **Jumbles: #1.** HAPPY **#2.** HOUSE **#3.** HUNTER **#4.** HOTTER **#5.** HAMMER **#6.** HOLIDAY
    Answer: HAMSTER

32. **Jumbles: #1.** BOSTON **#2.** PHOENIX **#3.** CHICAGO **#4.** SEATTLE **#5.** BUFFALO **#6.** ORLANDO
Answer: HOUSTON

33. **Jumbles: #1.** DUCK **#2.** FROG **#3.** MULE **#4.** OTTER **#5.** MOUSE **#6.** TURKEY
Answer: TURTLE

34. **Jumbles: #1.** BASE **#2.** CATCH **#3.** ERROR **#4.** INNING **#5.** STRIKE **#6.** TRIPLE
Answer: PITCHER

35. **Jumbles: #1.** REAGAN **#2.** HOOVER **#3.** WILSON **#4.** CLINTON **#5.** JOHNSON **#6.** COOLIDGE
Answer: LINCOLN

36. **Jumbles: #1.** CHAIR **#2.** BRICK **#3.** PHONE **#4.** FLOOR **#5.** OUTLET **#6.** GARAGE
Answer: CEILING

37. **Jumbles: #1.** GOLD **#2.** XENON **#3.** RADIUM **#4.** HELIUM **#5.** SILICON
Answer: ALUMINUM

38. **Jumbles: #1.** TIGER **#2.** RHINO **#3.** CAMEL **#4.** BEAVER **#5.** BABOON **#6.** WALRUS
Answer: RABBIT

39. **Jumbles: #1.** LIGHT **#2.** LUCKY **#3.** LOBBY **#4.** LESSON **#5.** LAWYER **#6.** LANTERN
Answer: LOGICAL

40. **Jumbles: #1.** CROW **#2.** EAGLE **#3.** STORK **#4.** CHICKEN **#5.** PENGUIN **#6.** VULTURE
Answer: PEACOCK

41. **Jumbles: #1.** BALL **#2.** DUNK **#3.** PUCK **#4.** GLOVE **#5.** ERROR **#6.** SEASON
Answer: DOUBLE

42. **Jumbles: #1.** OHIO **#2.** NEVADA **#3.** KANSAS **#4.** GEORGIA **#5.** WYOMING **#6.** KENTUCKY
Answer: WISCONSIN

43. **Jumbles: #1.** MATH **#2.** TARDY **#3.** PENCIL **#4.** LOCKER **#5.** ANSWER **#6.** SCIENCE
Answer: DIPLOMA

44. **Jumbles: #1.** UNCLE **#2.** INJURY **#3.** ABSENT **#4.** IMPACT **#5.** EUROPE **#6.** OREGON
Answer: OCTOBER

45. **Jumbles: #1.** PIANO **#2.** CHORD **#3.** TEMPO **#4.** MELODY **#5.** RHYTHM
Answer: HARMONY

46. **Jumbles: #1.** MIXED **#2.** MAINE **#3.** MAGIC **#4.** MOUTH **#5.** MITTEN **#6.** MOTION
Answer: MACHINE

47. **Jumbles: #1.** GRAF **#2.** COBB **#3.** AARON **#4.** PAYTON **#5.** JORDAN **#6.** NAMATH
Answer: MONTANA

48. **Jumbles: #1.** CUBA **#2.** EGYPT **#3.** FRANCE **#4.** GREECE **#5.** SWEDEN **#6.** VIETNAM
Answer: GERMANY

49. **Jumbles: #1.** PROP **#2.** STUNT **#3.** SCRIPT **#4.** STUDIO **#5.** WRITER **#6.** CAMERA
Answer: COSTUME

50. **Jumbles: #1.** RIVER **#2.** CRUST **#3.** WATER **#4.** ISLAND **#5.** JUNGLE **#6.** VOLCANO
Answer: CONTINENT

51. **Jumbles: #1.** DOWN **#2.** CATCH **#3.** BLOCK **#4.** TACKLE **#5.** FUMBLE **#6.** POSITION
Answer: TOUCHDOWN

52. **Jumbles: #1.** TYLER **#2.** ADAMS **#3.** WILSON **#4.** JACKSON **#5.** GARFIELD **#6.** BUCHANAN
Answer: HARDING

53. **Jumbles: #1.** EAGLE **#2.** SHEEP **#3.** PANDA **#4.** LIZARD **#5.** TURTLE **#6.** MONKEY
Answer: PENGUIN

54. **Jumbles: #1.** GLENN **#2.** COSBY **#3.** DISNEY **#4.** LENNON **#5.** POWELL **#6.** ROBERTS
Answer: PRESLEY

55. **Jumbles: #1.** SNOW **#2.** FLAKE **#3.** HUMID **#4.** BREEZE **#5.** CLOUDY **#6.** TWISTER
Answer: THUNDER

56. **Jumbles: #1.** ONE + THREE = FOUR **#2.** NINE – ONE = EIGHT **#3.** FIVE – FIVE = ZERO **#4.** SEVEN – FIVE = TWO **#5.** FOUR + THREE = SEVEN
Answer: FOUR + FOUR = EIGHT

57. **Jumbles: #1.** SULFUR **#2.** COPPER **#3.** HELIUM **#4.** TUNGSTEN **#5.** HYDROGEN
Answer: PLUTONIUM

58. **Jumbles: #1.** HUGE **#2.** SLIM **#3.** LUCKY **#4.** FUNNY **#5.** HAPPY **#6.** FRESH
Answer: GRUMPY

59. **Jumbles: #1.** GALAXY **#2.** SYSTEM **#3.** JUPITER **#4.** NEPTUNE **#5.** MERCURY **#6.** ASTEROID
Answer: SATURN

60. **Jumbles: #1.** PUNCH **#2.** POUND **#3.** PICKED **#4.** PAUSED **#5.** PUPPET **#6.** PRIVATE
Answer: PANCAKE

61. **Jumbles: #1.** LUNG **#2.** JOINT **#3.** BRAIN **#4.** THROAT **#5.** ENAMEL **#6.** EARDRUM
Answer: TONGUE

62. **Jumbles: #1.** SAFE RISKY **#2.** PLUS MINUS **#3.** SLIM THICK **#4.** GROW SHRINK **#5.** CHEER GLOOM
Answer: RICH POOR

63. **Jumbles: #1.** LISBON **#2.** BERLIN **#3.** LONDON **#4.** SYDNEY **#5.** MOSCOW **#6.** CHICAGO
Answer: MADRID

64. **Jumbles: #1.** BAND HAND **#2.** POUND ROUND **#3.** LOOSE NOOSE **#4.** LEDGE WEDGE **#5.** LETTER BETTER
Answer: HOUND BOUND

65. **Jumbles: #1.** EGYPT **#2.** RAILWAY **#3.** SEWING **#4.** ATLANTIC **#5.** OZONE **#6.** JAPAN
Answer: ESCALATOR

66. **Jumbles: #1.** KINGS **#2.** BULLS **#3.** EXPOS **#4.** MAGIC **#5.** GIANTS **#6.** COWBOYS
Answer: CELTICS

67. **Jumbles: #1.** DOVE **#2.** HAWK **#3.** EAGLE **#4.** PIGEON **#5.** TURKEY **#6.** OSTRICH
Answer: CARDINAL

68. **Jumbles: #1.** PILOT **#2.** AUTHOR **#3.** BARBER **#4.** DOCTOR **#5.** JANITOR **#6.** PLUMBER
Answer: REALTOR

69. **Jumbles: #1.** GREECE **#2.** POLAND **#3.** AUSTRIA **#4.** ENGLAND **#5.** HUNGARY **#6.** DENMARK
Answer: GERMANY

70. **Jumbles: #1.** ZINC **#2.** IRON **#3.** BORON **#4.** OXYGEN **#5.** COPPER **#6.** HELIUM
Answer: MERCURY

71. **Jumbles: #1.** HIVE **#2.** FARM **#3.** ADULT **#4.** APPLE **#5.** FENCE **#6.** GLASS
Answer: AIRPLANE

72. **Jumbles: #1.** SIGHT **#2.** SUDDEN **#3.** SPONGE **#4.** SEATTLE **#5.** SUSPECT **#6.** SCATTER
Answer: SUNSET

73. **Jumbles: #1.** FAIR **#2.** WIND **#3.** FRONT **#4.** STORM **#5.** BREEZE **#6.** TWISTER
Answer: RAINBOW

74. **Jumbles: #1.** FLORIDA **#2.** GEORGIA **#3.** WYOMING **#4.** MONTANA **#5.** VERMONT
Answer: DELAWARE

75. **Jumbles: #1.** RINK **#2.** STRIKE **#3.** ROOKIE **#4.** DEFEAT **#5.** FUMBLE **#6.** PITCHER
Answer: DEFENSE

76. **Jumbles: #1.** SKUNK **#2.** SHEEP **#3.** CHIMP **#4.** RABBIT **#5.** CHEETAH **#6.** RACCOON
Answer: PORCUPINE

77. **Jumbles: #1.** INDIA **#2.** KENYA **#3.** BRAZIL **#4.** FRANCE **#5.** DENMARK **#6.** PORTUGAL
Answer: ENGLAND

78. **Jumbles: #1.** SOCK **#2.** SHIRT **#3.** DRESS **#4.** FABRIC **#5.** BUTTON **#6.** MITTEN
Answer: UNIFORM

79. **Jumbles: #1.** BOSTON **#2.** PHOENIX **#3.** BISMARCK **#4.** COLUMBIA **#5.** HARTFORD
Answer: RICHMOND

80. **Jumbles: #1.** HIPPO **#2.** CAMEL **#3.** ZEBRA **#4.** GIRAFFE **#5.** BUFFALO **#6.** KANGAROO
Answer: PORCUPINE

81. **Jumbles: #1.** KIND **#2.** HARD **#3.** GOOD **#4.** HEAVY **#5.** ROUGH **#6.** MINOR
Answer: RANDOM

82. **Jumbles: #1.** PLUTO **#2.** GALAXY **#3.** HUBBLE **#4.** URANUS **#5.** JUPITER **#6.** MERCURY
Answer: SATELLITE

83. **Jumbles: #1.** BOSTON **#2.** MOBILE **#3.** DETROIT **#4.** HOUSTON **#5.** ORLANDO **#6.** MEMPHIS
Answer: SEATTLE

84. **Jumbles: #1.** COBALT **#2.** SODIUM **#3.** KRYPTON **#4.** MERCURY **#5.** CHLORINE
Answer: BISMUTH

85. **Jumbles: #1.** HAWAII **#2.** KANSAS **#3.** OREGON **#4.** FLORIDA **#5.** ARIZONA **#6.** VERMONT
Answer: OKLAHOMA

86. **Jumbles: #1.** SIX + ZERO = SIX **#2.** ONE + ZERO = ONE **#3.** SIX + SIX = TWELVE **#4.** EIGHT − ZERO = EIGHT **#5.** SEVEN + FOUR = ELEVEN
Answer: NINE − EIGHT = ONE

87. **Jumbles: #1.** TRUNK **#2.** GAUGE **#3.** ALARM **#4.** ENGINE **#5.** BUMPER **#6.** EXHAUST
Answer: GARAGE

88. **Jumbles: #1.** ALGAE **#2.** TRUNK **#3.** ORCHID **#4.** CACTUS **#5.** FLOWER **#6.** BAMBOO
Answer: BRANCH

89. **Jumbles: #1.** BILL **#2.** CASH **#3.** LOAN **#4.** WALLET **#5.** RECEIPT **#6.** ACCOUNT
Answer: INTEREST

90. **Jumbles: #1.** CAKE **#2.** APPLE **#3.** SNACK **#4.** CHEESE **#5.** WAFFLE **#6.** PUDDING
Answer: SANDWICH

91. **Jumbles: #1.** DEBATE **#2.** ENSLAVE **#3.** MIGHT **#4.** FIGHT **#5.** JUMBLE
Answer: LANGUAGE

92. **Jumbles: #1.** FISH **#2.** CRAB **#3.** TIGER **#4.** SKUNK **#5.** RABBIT **#6.** COUGAR
Answer: CHICKEN

93. **Jumbles: #1.** ONE × ZERO = ZERO
#2. ONE × FOUR = FOUR
#3. TEN + TEN = TWENTY
#4. ONE + SEVEN = EIGHT
#5. SIXTY ÷ TWO = THIRTY
Answer: TWO × FOUR = EIGHT

94. **Jumbles: #1.** STAY PRAY **#2.** HEDGE WEDGE **#3.** FROWN BROWN **#4.** POCKET LOCKET **#5.** BETTER SWEATER
Answer: NORWAY DOORWAY

95. **Jumbles: #1.** PACIFIC **#2.** ZEALAND **#3.** MACHINE **#4.** RADIO **#5.** ITALY **#6.** LENNON
Answer: FLORIDA

96. **Jumbles: #1.** IRON **#2.** GOLD **#3.** OXYGEN **#4.** COPPER **#5.** HELIUM **#6.** SODIUM
Answer: HYDROGEN

97. **Jumbles: #1.** BOISE **#2.** AUSTIN **#3.** JUNEAU **#4.** TOPEKA **#5.** LANSING **#6.** LINCOLN
Answer: BOSTON

98. **Jumbles: #1.** DAMP **#2.** FLOOD **#3.** ICICLE **#4.** DEGREE **#5.** THUNDER **#6.** FORECAST
Answer: RAINFALL

99. **Jumbles: #1.** WARSAW **#2.** SEATTLE **#3.** TORONTO **#4.** HOUSTON **#5.** GLASGOW **#6.** MONTREAL
Answer: LOS ANGELES

100. **Jumbles: #1.** HARRY **#2.** GEORGE **#3.** GROVER **#4.** MARTIN **#5.** DWIGHT **#6.** HERBERT
Answer: THEODORE

101. **Jumbles: #1.** THICK **#2.** TATTLE **#3.** TUXEDO **#4.** TROPHY **#5.** TRAFFIC **#6.** TONIGHT
Answer: TRACTOR

102. **Jumbles: #1.** JAPAN **#2.** JORDAN **#3.** FINLAND **#4.** BELGIUM **#5.** HUNGARY **#6.** MOROCCO
Answer: MONGOLIA

103. **Jumbles: #1.** BRAIN **#2.** CHEST **#3.** TOOTH **#4.** MOUTH **#5.** ARTERY **#6.** TONGUE
Answer: STOMACH

104. **Jumbles: #1.** APRIL **#2.** CABIN **#3.** SPEECH **#4.** LAWYER **#5.** DEBATE **#6.** KENTUCKY
Answer: PRESIDENT

105. **Jumbles: #1.** TAILOR **#2.** BUTLER **#3.** BROKER **#4.** CASHIER **#5.** SURGEON **#6.** JEWELER
Answer: WAITER

106. **Jumbles: #1.** CHILE **#2.** BRAZIL **#3.** MEXICO **#4.** SWEDEN **#5.** PANAMA **#6.** IRELAND **#7.** AUSTRIA
Answer: THAILAND

107. **Jumbles: #1.** FREELY **#2.** GLADLY **#3.** BOLDLY **#4.** POORLY **#5.** CALMLY **#6.** CLOSELY
Answer: LOCALLY

108. **Jumbles: #1.** ORBIT **#2.** COMET **#3.** APOLLO **#4.** SATURN **#5.** SYSTEM **#6.** KENNEDY
Answer: ASTEROID

109. **Jumbles: #1.** DOVE **#2.** PUMA **#3.** HYENA **#4.** OTTER **#5.** CHIMP **#6.** CAMEL
Answer: RACCOON

110. **Jumbles: #1.** TEST **#2.** FLUNK **#3.** LOCKER **#4.** LIBRARY **#5.** HISTORY **#6.** COLLEGE
Answer: SCIENCE

111. **Jumbles: #1.** FLAG **#2.** CABIN **#3.** PAPER **#4.** PENNY **#5.** HOBBY **#6.** BOOTH
Answer: ALPHABET

112. **Jumbles: #1.** HIGH LOFTY **#2.** HARM DAMAGE **#3.** HUGE IMMENSE **#4.** LOUSY ROTTEN **#5.** ERUPT EXPLODE
Answer: HOME HOUSE

113. **Jumbles: #1.** LION **#2.** TIGER **#3.** HYENA **#4.** JACKAL **#5.** BADGER **#6.** LEOPARD
Answer: POLAR BEAR

114. **Jumbles: #1.** EIGHT **#2.** EXACT **#3.** ENJOY **#4.** ORDER **#5.** IMPORT **#6.** ANSWER
Answer: AMERICA

115. **Jumbles: #1.** CHILE **#2.** RIVER **#3.** BRAZIL **#4.** AMAZON **#5.** BOLIVIA **#6.** ECUADOR
Answer: COLOMBIA

116. **Jumbles: #1.** VERB **#2.** VOICE **#3.** VIOLIN **#4.** VANISH **#5.** VANILLA **#6.** VIBRATE
Answer: VISITOR

117. **Jumbles: #1.** BEEF **#2.** COOKIE **#3.** BUTTER **#4.** MUFFIN **#5.** BANANA **#6.** OATMEAL
Answer: MEAT LOAF

118. **Jumbles: #1.** BANK **#2.** GOLD **#3.** VALUE **#4.** STOCK **#5.** INVEST **#6.** PAYMENT
Answer: SAVINGS

119. **Jumbles: #1.** FRANCE **#2.** POLAND **#3.** AUSTRIA **#4.** ROMANIA **#5.** BELGIUM **#6.** GERMANY
Answer: PORTUGAL

120. **Jumbles: #1.** FLUTE **#2.** POLKA **#3.** TEMPO **#4.** MAJOR **#5.** BASSOON
Answer: MEASURE

121. **Jumbles: #1.** FINCH **#2.** ROBIN **#3.** GOOSE **#4.** MALLARD **#5.** PARAKEET **#6.** FLAMINGO
Answer: OSTRICH

122. **Jumbles: #1.** PUNCH **#2.** HOMER **#3.** GOALIE **#4.** JERSEY **#5.** DOUBLE **#6.** CATCHER
Answer: STADIUM

123. **Jumbles: #1.** IDAHO **#2.** MAINE **#3.** OREGON **#4.** FLORIDA **#5.** MISSOURI **#6.** MICHIGAN
Answer: LOUISIANA

124. **Jumbles: #1.** HOOD **#2.** TRUCK **#3.** WIPER **#4.** WHEEL **#5.** DRIVER **#6.** PICKUP
Answer: VEHICLE

125. **Jumbles: #1.** HAIR **#2.** BONE **#3.** FOOT **#4.** GLAND **#5.** MOUTH **#6.** KIDNEY
Answer: ABDOMEN

126. **Jumbles: #1.** WALK **#2.** DUGOUT **#3.** DOUBLE **#4.** PITCHER **#5.** DIAMOND **#6.** MANAGER
Answer: BULL PEN

127. **Jumbles: #1.** ONE × FIVE = FIVE **#2.** SIX + SIX = TWELVE **#3.** THREE ÷ THREE = ONE **#4.** FOUR + FOUR = EIGHT **#5.** NINE + THREE = TWELVE
Answer: FOUR × FOUR = SIXTEEN

128. **Jumbles: #1.** OVEN **#2.** TABLE **#3.** PHONE **#4.** PANTRY **#5.** SWITCH **#6.** WINDOW
Answer: CABINET

129. **Jumbles: #1.** HIGH **#2.** FULL **#3.** WILD **#4.** SWIFT **#5.** LONELY **#6.** GLOSSY
Answer: HOLLOW

130. **Jumbles: #1.** MIAMI **#2.** OMAHA **#3.** DALLAS **#4.** ALBANY **#5.** SEATTLE **#6.** OAKLAND
Answer: ATLANTA

131. **Jumbles: #1.** LIBYA **#2.** KENYA **#3.** ZAMBIA **#4.** RWANDA **#5.** LIBERIA **#6.** MOROCCO
Answer: ZIMBABWE

132. **Jumbles: #1.** MINT **#2.** PENNY **#3.** POUND **#4.** INVEST **#5.** DOLLAR **#6.** CHARGE
Answer: TREASURY

133. **Jumbles: #1.** TREE **#2.** FERN **#3.** LIGHT **#4.** NEEDLE **#5.** BOTANY **#6.** CACTUS
Answer: FOLIAGE

134. **Jumbles: #1.** FRUIT **#2.** RELISH **#3.** BURGER **#4.** PEPPER **#5.** PRETZEL **#6.** SEAFOOD
Answer: SPAGHETTI

135. **Jumbles: #1.** RIVER **#2.** FAULT **#3.** BEACH **#4.** SWAMP **#5.** SEASON **#6.** MOUNTAIN
Answer: ATMOSPHERE

136. **Jumbles: #1.** OBOE **#2.** DRUM **#3.** FLUTE **#4.** VIOLIN **#5.** CORNET **#6.** BASSOON
Answer: TROMBONE

137. **Jumbles: #1.** BRAZIL **#2.** BOLIVIA **#3.** PACIFIC **#4.** URUGUAY **#5.** CARACAS **#6.** ATLANTIC
Answer: SANTIAGO

138. **Jumbles: #1.** APACHE **#2.** NAVAJO **#3.** PUEBLO **#4.** MOHAWK **#5.** MOHICAN **#6.** SHAWNEE
Answer: SEMINOLE

139. **Jumbles: #1.** IOWA **#2.** IDAHO **#3.** KANSAS **#4.** OREGON **#5.** ALABAMA
Answer: NEBRASKA

140. **Jumbles: #1.** DRESS **#2.** GLOVE **#3.** FABRIC **#4.** BUTTON **#5.** UNIFORM **#6.** SWEATER
Answer: GARMENT

141. **Jumbles: #1.** TIGERS **#2.** FLYERS **#3.** EAGLES **#4.** RAIDERS **#5.** PISTONS **#6.** WIZARDS
Answer: DODGERS

142. **Jumbles: #1.** CAVE **#2.** RIVER **#3.** GLOBE **#4.** VALLEY **#5.** JUNGLE **#6.** LAGOON
Answer: VOLCANO

143. **Jumbles: #1.** JAPAN **#2.** FRANCE **#3.** MEXICO **#4.** NIGERIA **#5.** JAMAICA **#6.** ENGLAND
Answer: IRELAND

144. **Jumbles: #1.** HYENA **#2.** CHIMP **#3.** LLAMA **#4.** MOOSE **#5.** COYOTE **#6.** GIRAFFE
Answer: PANTHER

145. **Jumbles: #1.** TAFT **#2.** POLK **#3.** ADAMS **#4.** REAGAN **#5.** LINCOLN **#6.** JOHNSON
Answer: JACKSON

146. **Jumbles: #1.** FOUR × ONE = FOUR **#2.** TWO × TEN = TWENTY **#3.** EIGHT ÷ ONE = EIGHT **#4.** ONE × ONE = ZERO + ONE **#5.** SIXTEEN × ZERO = ZERO
Answer: ZERO × TEN = TEN × ZERO

147. **Jumbles: #1.** CHILE **#2.** CANADA **#3.** MEXICO **#4.** PANAMA **#5.** NORWAY **#6.** BOLIVIA
Answer: MOROCCO

148. **Jumbles: #1.** DIMLY **#2.** NICELY **#3.** SOFTLY **#4.** FIRMLY **#5.** OPENLY **#6.** CRUDELY
Answer: PROUDLY

149. **Jumbles: #1.** HUSKY **#2.** BOXER **#3.** BEAGLE **#4.** SPANIEL **#5.** BULLDOG **#6.** SHEPHERD
Answer: GREYHOUND

150. **Jumbles: #1.** BIRD **#2.** KING **#3.** BORG **#4.** BENCH **#5.** BERRA **#6.** HOGAN
Answer: GEHRIG

151. **Jumbles: #1.** PANAMA **#2.** AFRICA **#3.** CRISIS **#4.** POCKET **#5.** BRITISH **#6.** POLAND
Answer: COMPACT DISC

152. **Jumbles: #1.** INDIA **#2.** SYRIA **#3.** RUSSIA **#4.** VIETNAM **#5.** PAKISTAN **#6.** MONGOLIA
Answer: SINGAPORE

153. **Jumbles: #1.** TAFT **#2.** FORD **#3.** ARTHUR **#4.** REAGAN **#5.** HOOVER **#6.** JOHNSON
Answer: JEFFERSON

154. **Jumbles: #1.** SLOWLY **#2.** NOTICE **#3.** REALIZE **#4.** BRAND **#5.** SECOND
Answer: CALENDAR

155. **Jumbles: #1.** SOSA **#2.** TWAIN **#3.** WOODS **#4.** JORDAN **#5.** MARTIN **#6.** HOUSTON
Answer: MADONNA

156. **Jumbles: #1.** IODINE **#2.** COPPER **#3.** HELIUM **#4.** SODIUM **#5.** URANIUM **#6.** MERCURY
Answer: CALCIUM

157. **Jumbles: #1.** LUNAR **#2.** URANUS **#3.** SYSTEM **#4.** AURORA **#5.** ECLIPSE **#6.** GRAVITY
Answer: UNIVERSE

158. **Jumbles: #1.** JUNIOR **#2.** AVENUE **#3.** AUGUST **#4.** PARKWAY **#5.** SATURDAY **#6.** NOVEMBER
Answer: MOUNTAIN

159. **Jumbles: #1.** BRAIN **#2.** CHEST **#3.** BLOOD **#4.** KIDNEY **#5.** SPLEEN **#6.** TONGUE
Answer: BACKBONE

160. **Jumbles: #1.** RICH POOR **#2.** DARK LIGHT **#3.** FULL EMPTY **#4.** BASE SUMMIT **#5.** WIDE NARROW
Answer: EASY HARD

161. **Jumbles: #1.** WEDGE **#2.** WRENCH **#3.** WISHFUL **#4.** WEDDING **#5.** WEEKDAY **#6.** WELCOME
Answer: WOUNDED

162. **Jumbles: #1.** SYDNEY **#2.** LONDON **#3.** BOMBAY **#4.** WARSAW **#5.** CHICAGO **#6.** HOUSTON
Answer: BAGHDAD

163. **Jumbles: #1.** PARKA **#2.** DRESS **#3.** JEANS **#4.** JACKET **#5.** SANDAL **#6.** MITTEN
Answer: SNEAKER

164. **Jumbles: #1.** ASIA **#2.** IDAHO **#3.** UNION **#4.** ADULT **#5.** UNFAIR **#6.** ORANGE
Answer: ENGLAND

165. **Jumbles: #1.** GLAND **#2.** PELVIS **#3.** THORAX **#4.** TENDON **#5.** MUSCLE **#6.** TRACHEA
Answer: EARDRUM

166. **Jumbles: #1.** BOOK **#2.** TRUCK **#3.** WORLD **#4.** WAGON **#5.** TICKET **#6.** OFFICE
Answer: BUILDING

167. **Jumbles: #1.** CRAB **#2.** MOLE **#3.** STORK **#4.** COYOTE **#5.** GORILLA **#6.** PANTHER
Answer: CHICKEN

168. **Jumbles: #1.** TAMPA **#2.** DALLAS **#3.** BOSTON **#4.** DETROIT **#5.** SEATTLE **#6.** ATLANTA
Answer: BALTIMORE

169. **Jumbles: #1.** LEVEL **#2.** RUSTY **#3.** STEEP **#4.** YOUNG **#5.** LITTLE **#6.** RANDOM
Answer: GENTLE

170. **Jumbles: #1.** FRENCH **#2.** MARTHA **#3.** VICTORY **#4.** COUNTRY **#5.** VIRGINIA **#6.** DELAWARE
Answer: MOUNT VERNON

171. **Jumbles: #1.** CURVE **#2.** SKIING **#3.** TENNIS **#4.** TROPHY **#5.** FAIRWAY **#6.** MANAGER
Answer: UNIFORM

172. **Jumbles: #1.** HAIL **#2.** MILD **#3.** CHILLY **#4.** CYCLONE **#5.** DROUGHT **#6.** BLIZZARD
Answer: CLIMATE

173. **Jumbles: #1.** MIND **#2.** LAWNS **#3.** WHILE **#4.** GROW **#5.** SPRING
Answer: SEASON

174. **Jumbles: #1.** ZINC **#2.** GOLD **#3.** SULFUR **#4.** OXYGEN **#5.** COBALT **#6.** SILICON
Answer: NITROGEN

175. **Jumbles: #1.** PANDA **#2.** JAGUAR **#3.** FERRET **#4.** GORILLA **#5.** MUSKRAT **#6.** ELEPHANT
Answer: REINDEER

176. **Jumbles: #1.** INDIA **#2.** PANAMA **#3.** NIGERIA **#4.** AUSTRIA **#5.** ICELAND **#6.** DENMARK
Answer: PAKISTAN

177. **Jumbles: #1.** SKUNK **#2.** CAMEL **#3.** RABBIT **#4.** TURTLE **#5.** GOPHER **#6.** MONKEY
Answer: CHIPMUNK

178. **Jumbles: #1.** FOUR $\div$ TWO = TWO **#2.** SIX $\div$ TWO = THREE **#3.** ONE $\times$ SEVEN = SEVEN **#4.** THREE $\times$ THREE = NINE **#5.** FIVE $\times$ TWO = TEN + ZERO
Answer: ONE $\times$ ONE = FIVE − FOUR

179. **Jumbles: #1.** BOISE **#2.** ALBANY **#3.** PHOENIX **#4.** ATLANTA **#5.** JACKSON **#6.** CONCORD
Answer: LINCOLN